Mourning
to Morning

Mourning to Morning

A book about grief, death, heaven and healing.

LINDA BLECHINGER

authorHOUSE®

AuthorHouse™
1663 Liberty Drive
Bloomington, IN 47403
www.authorhouse.com
Phone: 1-800-839-8640

Published by AuthorHouse   07/30/2012

ISBN: 978-1-4772-5527-8 (sc)
ISBN: 978-1-4772-5526-1 (hc)
ISBN: 978-1-4772-5528-5 (e)

Library of Congress Control Number: 2012913982

✍ CONTENTS

ॐ DEDICATION

This book is dedicated to the love of my life, my husband, Daniel—You were Jesus' hands and feet to me and His eyes and mouth. God used you to reveal Jesus to me. I am eternally grateful and forever changed because of you. You love me so well. You are the wind beneath my wings.

To my sons Derek and David—I couldn't possibly express my immense love for you both. You are a constant source of delight and inspiration. Thank you so much for the encouragement along the way. This book is as much for the two of you as it is for all those who have experienced what our family has. I love you! Derek, thank you for the beautiful cover!

To my family members, friends and Pastors—Each of you has enriched our lives in beautiful ways. My heart is full of gratitude as I think of each of you—thank you!

To my parents and in-laws—See you in heaven—I love you!

✑ ACKNOWLEDGMENTS

Thank you to Kim, Sheila and Susan—Your input and direction were invaluable to me!

A huge thank you to my editor, Cheryl Lewis—You took on this project of a rewrite to my original book, giving your heart to it as though you knew our precious DJ. I will always remember our time together at your cabin in the mountains, crying, praying and writing! Thank you so very much. You are a gem!

I truly thank my Lord Jesus Christ—You saved me, You delivered me, You made me brand new. You have carried me when I couldn't take another step. You comforted me when no one could. You are my light and salvation, my very present help in time of need. One day I know we will all be reunited. Until that day, I live to serve You. Eternally yours, your daughter, Linda

🖤 INTRODUCTION

This book is written with the intention of helping individuals—perhaps family members, or friends of those who have experienced loss and are grieving. Our hope is that it will lend insight into the days, weeks, months and, yes, even years of grieving and healing.

We pray that God uses our story to encourage you as you make your way through these deep waters. Mainly, we desire to share with you God's faithfulness. Scripture tells us King David mourned over the death of his son; Jesus wept for Lazarus, His friend; Elijah responded to the cry of a desperate mother. Dan and I mourned the death of our precious son DJ, all the while still trying to comfort and help our sons, Derek and David understand and deal with the loss of their brother. Ecclesiastes says, *There is a time to be born and a time to die, a time to laugh and a time to cry.*

Our message to you: It is okay to cry, weep, mourn, grieve—you are supposed to. It is normal. Everyone grieves in his or her own way—there is not a right or wrong way to grieve. We are all individuals. Just know you will not cry daily forever. Your heart will begin to heal. God is faithful. He will see you through, just as He has done for our family.

CHAPTER ONE
A MOTHER'S ACCOUNT

When I started this journey, the potential for devastating loss was the last thing on my mind. In fact, life was downright wonderful!

Dan and I met on my birthday March 3rd, 1987. We met at work—he was an engineer and I was a manager for rework, final inspection and shipping in a printed-circuit manufacturer on Long Island. Dan had moved down to Long Island from Upstate NY after graduating from RIT. He was 6'2 with eyes of blue—a dashing young man, full of energy and smiles. He played basketball and baseball, yet he was the consummate gentleman!

When Dan first asked me out on a date, I said, "No, I don't need any more trouble in my life!" I laugh at that statement now, because he was not dissuaded, but very persistent!

One day at work, I received a phone call from one of my sisters that my mother was en route to the hospital. She was apparently hemorrhaging and they didn't know if she would make it to the hospital alive. At that point in my life, I had a tumultuous relationship with my mother and we hadn't spoken in quite some time, so I was feeling conflicted and upset. I did something quite uncharacteristic: I called Dan at his office and told him the news I had just received. In a flash, there he was, standing in my office with his coat on and keys in his hands saying, "Come on, Linda. I'm driving you to the hospital." I halfheartedly argued, but he won and, before I knew it, we were on the road.

While we were driving to Port Jefferson, Dan asked me if he could pray for my mom. I hesitantly agreed, because I had never heard anyone pray outside of church, never mind in a car! I was amazed by how he just seemed to talk to God as though they were best friends. It stirred something in me.

Later that evening, when we knew mom was safe, we made our way home. Dan shared stories of his childhood during the drive, and he also told me how he knew Jesus! I mean he actually said he personally knew Him. I didn't ask any questions. I just listened and somehow it was enough—when I was back at my apartment that very night, I asked God to do for me what He did for Dan. I wanted to personally KNOW Jesus! It was a night I will never forget—alone with God, I accepted Jesus Christ!

When Dan proposed to me on the 4th of July in 1987, only four months after we met, he slipped an engagement ring—with one round diamond in the middle and three baguettes to the left—on my finger and looked into my eyes.

"This diamond represents you, Linda, and the three small diamonds represent our three boys," he said.

I joyfully accepted and chuckled at this man who was so sure this was the way it would be. I had to admit that, thus far, everything else he had planned for his life was right on schedule. He had decided by the time he was 17 where he wanted to go to college (he went there), that he would leave the farm and live in the city (he was on Long Island) and knew he would meet the girl he would marry, have a house and be married by the time he was 25. He told me all of this on our first date. He was 24 and, before he turned 25, we were married.

It was the happiest day of my life. We were married in Pulaski, the little upstate New York town in which Dan had grown up. It was July. I felt there couldn't be a more perfect day in all of history! If you have never been there, let me tell you the colors are stunning and the weather ideal. Family and friends gathered around as we celebrated all weekend. Our honeymoon was a whirlwind, just like our romance!

Dan was and is still my night in shining armor—the prince who swept me off my feet, the love of my life!

When I received the news I was pregnant, I slipped a note in Dan's office without him seeing me. It said on the front, "Congratulations!" and, on the inside, "Daddy." I waited at my desk for the phone call and, sure enough, within minutes it came. He was very excited, just as I knew he would be, and he kept asking, "Are you sure?" It was a wonderful time in our lives. Together, we planned for our baby, dreamed of how the baby would look and thought of names. We shared the happy news with our family members and then we started discussing where we would live. If we stayed on Long Island, I would have to continue to work, so Dan asked me to come with him on a trip to Georgia to explore the possibility of moving from New York. At the time, he was traveling to Peachtree City about twice a month for work. So, we went house hunting in Georgia and fell in love with the little city of Newnan. Georgia was now our home. We made the move when I was nine months pregnant. That was a bold step, but we were anxious to begin getting acclimated. June in Georgia while nine months pregnant—can you imagine?! That pretty much sums it up!

Our first son, Derek, was born June of 1989. We cried as we thanked God for this precious, beautiful gift. Derek was amazing to me—wide eyed from the beginning, looking around as if to say, "OK, world, here I am!"

He was a true delight. I remember talking and singing to him all the time. Dan and I had fun as we prepared a bright nursery for Derek—yellow like the sunshine, with Sesame Street characters and ABCs all around the room. I made the curtains by hand—my first attempt at such things. I just loved being a mom. I had worked since I was 15. I was now 29, so this was definitely a new page in my life and I wholly embraced it. I actually had not known life could be so wonderful! Every day seemed to hold new surprises and adventures.

Dan and I shared the parenting responsibilities. Derek was pretty easygoing—just always hungry. I found that everything about being a mom agreed with me. I watched in absolute wonder as this little baby grew, his personality developing right along with his body. I delighted in his every achievement. I listened to him "talking" endlessly to me and we read together several times throughout each day.

I never knew my heart could hold so much love! Derek had blue eyes and blonde hair, long eyelashes and a charming smile. Full of curiosity and ever discovering new treasures, my son stole my heart!

Four months later, I discovered I was pregnant, again. We were overjoyed! He was already named before he was born. Though I wanted to name him Dean, Dan said no. He wanted the name to be "Douglas," so it was: Douglas Jacob Blechinger! His middle name was after Dan's grandfather and I liked it quite well. Dan also wanted to call him "DJ," honoring his lifelong friend Don, who was nicknamed DJ.

By the time he was expected to arrive, the bassinet for DJ was in our room. We received another crib and so had the new nursery ready for our second son.

The time finally arrived. It was a blistering-hot summer day at the end of July. We were very eager, as our second son was about to make his entrance into the world. We had prepared for this day and it was finally here. Derek had just turned 1 year old the month before and was excited about being a big brother.

I loved being pregnant both times, but this was special, because Derek was such a part of praying for this baby. I know that it is hard to believe a 1 year old would be talking and praying, but he did. I have a video of him running around and talking at his first birthday party. He loved praying with us! Derek was already very astute and seemed keenly aware of people, emotions and even the "spiritual atmosphere" of his surroundings.

My mom was visiting from New York just in time for our second son's big arrival. Mom adored babies and was very excited to be part of DJ's entrance. Finally, the labor pangs began! My water broke and off to the hospital we went. We were so excited!

All went like clockwork. That was a relief, because Derek's delivery had been a 72-hour ordeal. I can honestly say I labored for that child! (He was worth it!)

DJ was a totally different story. I remember the nurse coming in to check on me and saying, "Oh, honey, you have plenty of time. Why don't you get up and walk around for a bit to get things moving?" She smiled as she left the room.

I managed to get up out of that contraption they call a bed, so that I could use the restroom but, as soon as I stood up, I felt the baby drop. I knew what that feeling meant! There was no doubt in my mind as I said, with complete control, "Dan, go get the nurse. The baby is coming!"

Of course, my precious husband began to remind me, "The nurse just checked you, honey." I didn't need to say much more—my look of "Get her now or die!" was very convincing.

The nurse, probably also assuming I was overeager, sauntered in and obligingly lifted the sheet. To her astonishment, she saw what I already knew—DJ was entering the world!

"Don't push!" she yelled.

Don't push? Was she serious? She and Dan began racing my bed down the hall to the O.R. and I wasn't especially happy about the prospect of delivering my baby there—but I wasn't really in a position to argue! There stood Dr. Steigleman—one glove on and one glove off. Before he could say, "Don't push yet," DJ was born!

No anesthesia. No epidural.

He was a beautiful 7-lb, 6-ounce baby boy—perfect in every way! I held him and kissed him, looking into his dark blue eyes that looked as though they would soon be brown just like mine! He was beautiful!

I remember being a little concerned that he didn't want to nurse, but everyone said he was fine. Proud Daddy held his second son, again thanking God for such a blessing. He kissed DJ's head and we looked into each other's eyes, filled with all of the amazement we had also felt during the birth of our first son.

DJ was a living, breathing miracle from God! Dan handed him to the nurse, so they could do all the cleaning up and such. It was going to be a little while until we all three would be together, again, so Dan left the hospital to go home and tell Derek and mom all the events of the past three hours. He was planning to soon bring them to see DJ. My world could not have been more perfect! I couldn't wait to hold DJ again!

Have you ever wished you could freeze a moment in time and not move toward what happened next?

When the pediatrician came into my room and said she was trying to get in touch with Dan and had tried unsuccessfully to call my husband at home, I felt the blood drain from my face. My hearing became very concentrated as I evaluated her face and tone of voice. I felt compelled to ask the question, but was terrified of the answer. I spoke through a constricted throat, "Dr. Warren is something wrong with my baby? Please . . . you need to tell me now." Jasmina Warren was more than our pediatrician; she was a friend and confidant. I knew her and felt comfortable with her typically direct-although-loving approach, which suited me fine. Now, she was reserved and her words seemed carefully measured.

She really didn't want to talk to me without Dan being present, but I insisted. I couldn't wait—I had to know. Every part of my being was focused on knowing.

"Linda, your son has a heart defect," she said. "I think it's pretty severe."

I was stunned. I just sat there staring at her. My mouth was parched and my mind was racing. What was she saying? Was he going to die? How serious was it? A heart defect—what did that mean? *A defect* . . . I kept hearing those words.

I didn't say a word, but it seemed as though she knew all the questions raging through my mind.

"I don't know exactly what is wrong," she said. "I believe it is pretty serious, but listen. I do know they can do surgery for all kinds of heart defects. Don't give up hope. I know a great cardiologist at Egleston and a great pediatric heart surgeon. We need to get DJ there as soon as we can. I'm going back in to him now to prepare him for transport." She concluded, "When Dan gets here, I will speak to him. Tell him to ask for me." Dr. Warren explained the procedure that she was going to perform to prepare DJ for transport on *Angel One*, the life-support mobile unit that would bring our precious new baby to Egleston. She assembled a team of professionals that worked with her. She left the room to take care of my baby.

In shock and distress, I made the call to Dan at home and told him to come back to the hospital—something was wrong with our baby.

Dan hung up and raced back to the hospital.

When Dan arrived at the hospital and walked into my room, I finally cried. Dan held me for a moment, comforting me, but I knew he needed to talk with Dr. Warren, so I sent him to her. He went in to our pediatrician and, as she was working meticulously on our precious DJ, she explained again all she had come to understand about DJ's situation.

Dan wanted to arrive at Egleston before DJ and the ambulance did, so that all the papers would be signed and there would be no conceivable delays.

I told him that I would be fine. "Just go and take care of our baby."

When they had DJ all prepared for transport, the woman who was to travel with him brought in my sweet little boy. He was in a portable incubator. I knew it was necessary—this was life and death. It seemed so sterile and so isolating for him. They brought him into my room so I could say good-bye. In fact, I was told he may not make it to Egleston. Somehow, I knew that wasn't true, that he would make it to the hospital and I would see him again. I don't know how to explain that mindset. Was it sheer determination, wishful thinking, a lack of knowledge or trust in my God?

I thank God that we did not know all that was to come. The understanding would have been too much to handle emotionally. With my precious baby and Dan gone, I cried and prayed and cried some more. I had a uterine tear from my swift labor and delivery and I had lost too much blood to be released. It was agony to be apart from my new son. He was so small and fragile.

I opened the Gideon Bible on the nightstand to Psalm 91: 1-4. It read:

> *"He who dwells in the shelter of the most High will abide in the shadow of the Almighty. I will say to the LORD, 'My refuge and my Fortress, my God in whom I trust!' For it is He who delivers you from the snare of the trapper and from the deadly pestilence. He will cover you with His pinions, and under His wings you may seek refuge; His faithfulness is a shield and a bulwark."*

God is so good. He knew I needed a promise and I took it as my own.

"God, I believe You," I said, through my tears. "You have to take care of our baby. Please, Lord, let me see him. Let him live."

When DJ arrived at Egleston, all had been prepared for him. They immediately brought him to the Catheter Lab and performed a ballooned septectomy on his aorta to open the aorta, the vessel that carries oxygenated blood to the rest of the body. This was a successful procedure and so we had our first victory.

Of course, I was still at the hospital in Newnan and cried through the night. Eventually, a nurse came in and asked if I wanted something to help me sleep. I said no but, when she urged, "If you take this, it will help you sleep and be rested and ready for tomorrow," I changed my mind. I knew I would never sleep on my own since, every time I heard a baby cry, I cried, too.

I drifted off to a hard and fretful night of sleep. Morning finally came and, miraculously, my blood work came back normal. With Dan again by my side, I was released from the hospital. I had one thought: I could see my baby!

Though I was walking slowly down that hallway, since I wasn't physically able to walk any faster, my heart was racing. Dan helped me balance as we approached the NICU. There he was—our second diamond—so tiny, so helpless, and laying there asleep. Everything seemed surreal, like a space-age scene. Monitors, screens, pumps and wires were all hooked up to my baby. I looked at his little fingers—so small, so fragile, and so perfect. I thought, "How can it be? How can his heart not be just as perfect?" The sign the nurses made for him (I still have it) says, "DJ" with a smile in the crook of the J. It was a personal touch that softened the sight.

That's when I met DJ's cardiologist, a tall man with a deep voice. His eyes said to me, "I care about your baby and I'm going to do everything I can to help." I was comforted. He was very truthful from the beginning and I needed that. I also needed to know he would be candid with us.

The doctor drew pictures for us of DJ's heart and used a small model of a heart to explain the different defects. He took his time with us and shared that DJ needed a medical procedure called a Fontan, but that the surgeon, and he agreed, wanted to wait as long as possible to do that surgery, so that DJ could first grow.

His little body needed to be bigger and stronger. The heart is an incredible organ, very complex—we had a lot to learn.

When DJ's heart surgeon came in, I knew immediately that God had chosen these two men. I felt such a deep peace. Dan confirmed that he felt the same as we talked and prayed about the doctors. They gave us a lot of choices to make and, when we prayed about it, we felt God was telling us to trust them.

I stayed with DJ at the hospital, day and night, as Dan went home to care for Derek. It was difficult, but we felt it was extremely important for Derek to see as much of us as possible. We tried to keep his home schedule the same, since he was only 13 months old. Dan would bring Derek up to the hospital on weekends to visit momma and baby brother DJ, which was quite a trek for poor Dan, loading up diapers and bottles, snacks and toys. Dan was trying to keep some sense of normalcy in the midst of this new turbulence that was thrust upon us.

Meanwhile, I learned about the IV pumps, monitors, syringes and medicines. I bathed DJ every day. I sang to him. I prayed for him.

Slowly, I began to realize there were other babies on that floor that had no one. Their parents had abandoned them. I was brokenhearted for these little ones and began to hold and pray for them, too.

We met parents of the ailing babies and children on the heart floor. I began to be able to tell the new ones from the parents who had been there before. Like me, the new parents at the hospital had the look of disbelief and fear. The mothers all looked ill themselves and the fathers looked like warriors that didn't know whom to fight.

Dan and I were very touched by the need for family counseling. Many couples were not able to stand together through these trials; instead, we saw the strain and stress driving them apart. Dan would often speak with the husbands and I would speak with the wives, encouraging them not to give up hope or each other.

Life in the hospital is a totally different world. Sleeping on a cot, eating in the cafeteria, watching the world continue to carry on normally—it was strange. I remember walking down the hallway in my pajamas, heading toward the shower carrying fresh clothes and assorted items and thinking, "Wow, Linda Blechinger, who wouldn't be caught in public without being fully dressed, make-up on, hair done, is tromping down the hallway of this huge hospital, not caring who sees me." My only true goal was to leave the hospital, my driving question: When will DJ be well enough for us to go home, so we can be a normal family, again? I so desired to be with my family and for DJ to experience family life in his own safe home.

Day after day and night after night, you are face to face with illness, surgery and death. Little victories are celebrated by all. Everyone cheers as you leave to go home, as though you're not ever coming back—but you know the truth is you will be back and you will probably see everyone sooner rather then later. Still, for now, you're going home and it is a reason to celebrate!

⚜ CHAPTER TWO
WHAT IS NORMAL?

The first time we were able to take DJ home was thrilling—and terrifying!

In the hospital, of course, there were heart monitors and pulse oxygen machines. The nurses came in every two hours to check on him and blood work was regularly drawn from his IV. If he needed a test, it was scheduled within hours and we would talk to the doctors daily. When we were told we could take DJ home, I panicked. Of course, I wanted this more than anything. To go home meant seeing and holding my Derek, sleeping in my own bed, eating my own cooking, putting DJ down in his own crib surrounded by love and comfort—sanctuary! But this whole prospect became daunting. Would I really be able to care for him the way he needed? What if I missed something or didn't realize he needed help? He was so little—barely more than a month old—with four medicines, three times a day.

The nurses all assured me that I was capable of caring for him at home and that we would have access to them if we needed them. Still, I was nervous. When we were finally home, I remember not wanting to leave his side and not wanting to sleep at night. I would watch his chest rise and fall, listening for any little sound that seemed abnormal. I made a chart with all of the times and medicines listed. I had alarms set "just in case."

Slowly, I began to trust that I would remember his schedule. As DJ grew, I could literally look into his eyes and see if he was uncomfortable, in pain, hungry or laboring to breathe, I learned to use a stethoscope and count breaths. Some things became second nature, but some were dreadful and I hated having to do them to my son.

I learned to route a feeding tube down his tiny nasal passage into his stomach. Poor DJ, of course, hated this done to him and he would often cry when he saw the feeding tube. He knew I had to put it in. I loathed having to do this to him, but he absolutely had to have nourishment and this was the only way. I would try not to cry, but just reassure him. It was almost over as soon as I laid him down to start the procedure. After a while, it was impossible to put the tube down his nasal passage. The area had become scarred and thickened and so came the time for the surgery that enabled DJ to be fed directly into his stomach—without the dreaded nasal feeding tube. I learned to clean and dress his G-tube (Gastric-Tube) when he had the fundoplication procedure.

I became knowledgeable in detecting when he needed his dose of Lasix increased, because he was building up fluid around his heart. I learned chest PTs and basic physical therapy techniques to help strengthen his muscles after surgeries or long periods in bed.

I learned things I never wanted to know or dreamed I would need to know as a mom! I did them, because it meant a chance at life for my DJ. I now know I would have done whatever it took for him.

During this period, we had many wonderful times—memories that are priceless. There were difficult times, of course, but Derek and DJ were a true enjoyment.

After much prayer and against the advice of concerned doctors, we had our third son—our third diamond, David Robert, born in February of 1992. DJ was delighted to now also be a big brother like Derek!

While I was pregnant, Derek and DJ would rub my belly and melodiously say, "Davey, can you hear me? We love you!"

Our family was now complete (and so was Dan's prediction)—three boys!

The years passed quickly, as they do when you have small children. Derek and DJ were great helpers with "their" baby. Every time David would cry, DJ would say, "I get him" and Derek and DJ would race to David's rescue and try to comfort him with their pacifiers. David never took a pacifier, but DJ was just sure he needed one, anyway. The boys were all very close.

DJ loved to kiss David's forehead. Every time I sat David down, there was DJ kissing him. Derek and DJ would be "clowns" and "bees" and "sonic" and anything they could think of to get David laughing. It didn't take much. Dave was enamored with his big brothers. If he dared let out a whimper, the dynamic duo instantly appeared!

When Derek started kindergarten, it was a huge event for our family. DJ was so excited that he would ask me all day, "What is Derek doing now, Mommy? Is he reading? Is he coloring? Is he playing? Does he miss me?"

DJ would sit at home and pretend he was in school, too. At 2 years old, David was the perfect student. DJ would tell David to play or sing or read and David would do his best to make his brother proud. What an adorable memory!

Once a week—sometimes twice—I went up to Derek's school with the other two boys and we would all enjoy story time together. DJ would crack us up, because he would approach the prettiest girl in the reading circle and ask sweetly if he could sit next to her or in her lap. Actually, he wasn't much younger, but he was tiny and very cute and sweet. They always said yes! His eyes twinkled with delight, simply because he could be in school with his brother and participate.

Mrs. Maddox, Derek's teacher, was kind and loving to the children. They adored her and my three sons were no different. When it was time to pick up Derek from school, we waited in the carpool line outside and sang songs as we watched the other kids come out of the building. We would compete to see who could see Derek first.

One afternoon, Derek was upset. A classmate had been mean to him and he was recounting the whole wretched thing to me when DJ piped up from his seat in the back of the van, "Derek, I will scratch her. She made you cry. She is bad!"

We all laughed about DJ's reaction and it is still a favorite family remembrance.

DJ had four surgeries in his first year of life. In fact, we had a "celebration of life" service at our church, Grace Community Fellowship in Newnan, in honor of the Lord's goodness in DJ's life and in ours. During his first year, he had the first ballooned septectomy, two heart surgeries and one skull surgery.

Each time he went into surgery, I asked the Lord, "Will he make it, Lord? Please let me know." I always had an inward peace that he would pull through and, each time, he did.

DJ was so sweet to everyone, but had a killer screech each time the poor phlebotomist came in to draw blood. Those lungs were exercised but, when they finished, through big alligator tears, DJ would say, "Thank you." It reduced them to cry with him every time.

DJ would often ask for "his" nurses. There were three he particularly favored. They were wonderful to all of us. They were like little rays of sunshine in some pretty intense storms. Of course, there were battles with some hospital personnel and things could get pretty passionate on both the parent side and the professional side. Dealing with life and death on a day-to-day basis is emotionally taxing. I learned I was DJ's advocate and the one who had to voice my questions and concerns about his care. I knew what his little moans and groans meant. I could judge how he was feeling, even when he couldn't tell me. Somehow, a mother can just *feel* when something is wrong with her child and, when the child is terminally ill, they learn at an even deeper level. A look in his eyes, the color of his fingers or nose, the tones of a cry or worse the lack of a cry, and his sleep pattern . . . I was on constant watch. Always "tuned in."

I loved most of the nurses and doctors. They treated DJ like a person, rather than just another case. The ones who were the best and had the most impact on us as a family were the nurses and doctors who listened to concerns, wanted parents involved and recognized us as the ultimate authority over our son. They cared about all of us as a family and I will never forget them.

I hated when I was made to feel like I was in the way, which was rare but, when it happened, wow—emotions felt raw! The few that had that attitude made me feel like taking DJ and leaving. There was more than one occasion when I came close to doing just that. Once trust was established, things went smoothly—even when, medically, they weren't going as we had hoped. We trusted DJ's doctors, who knew his heart and medical needs. We worked through the bumps in the road. It's kind of like extended family—we must learn to get along. Not everyone likes everyone else. Personalities can get in the way, so I had to make a decision: As long as I felt their attitude toward my son was for the best and they were doing their job, I just had to tolerate those who, in my opinion, should have chosen a different profession. I tried to remember they had to face these medical issues, children and parents every day, but somehow that made me feel all the more that they should understand the fragile emotions from our perspective.

Once, a nurse told me she was sure I didn't understand the pressure that *they* were under every day, facing life and death—that it was *more* difficult on them, because it was their profession. I had no tolerance for this at the time because, in my mind, they chose their profession. They could choose to leave. The children and their parents certainly did not choose to be there and could not really choose to leave. As the families and staff in the hospital bond and get to know each other, we join in each other's victories and defeats and, yes, even in sorrows. I do pray for hospital staff, because I know they truly do face a very difficult job. However, I don't accept this as an excuse for a poor attitude toward parents or, especially, patients. In any case, the general attitude of the medical staff was positive and supportive. When you are under continual emotional duress and sleep deprivation, the bad attitudes seem magnified. I thank God for DJ's special nurses, Holly, Lori and Karen. They will always hold a special place in our hearts. There were many other nurses that were also kind, but these three were extra special.

We had very hard times, both medically and financially, but we also had precious times of laughter and playing, drawing and playdough, days at the park and playing in the water sprinklers, bubbles, star gazing, collecting leaves and baking cookies. We relished every moment. Every holiday was special. Friends and family gave us strength.

So many times, I was emotionally drained and that's exactly when I would receive an encouraging card or note. My mother-in-law flew down when we had a scheduled surgery for DJ and took the boys for walks and sang songs to them. They loved to hear her read stories to them. It seemed Mom always made us feel better about leaving, knowing she was at home. God met us in every difficulty.

We had dear friends nearby who functioned like family, since we had no relatives in the area. At the time, they didn't have children of their own, so they showered our boys with attention and affection. Our friends loved our boys and our boys loved our friends. We went to church with Paul and Karen Anderson and became very close with them. I thank God for Karen. She learned all about DJ's medications, she knew how to work his feeding pump and keep him on his schedule. I can remember so well DJ looking into Karen's eyes, exclaiming, "And you know what?!" and Karen replying with just as much excitement, "What, DJ?!"

God truly blessed us with our friends. We had Bible studies in our home, shared meals together and prayed together. Indeed, our church family was just that—family. The women of the church became our friends and seemed, as they met our needs, our very own aunts, grandmothers and mothers. We laughed and cried together. I knew they constantly prayed for us and, in fact, I know they still do.

I remember when DJ was about 4 months old and finally home. The women had a baby shower for him and I cried as they acknowledged the life of my precious little boy. When DJ was born, word spread very quickly that something was wrong with him—something very serious. No one knew whether he would live or die. People didn't know what to do. I'm sure they wrestled with the right thing to do—but the outcome was that we didn't receive any congratulation cards or acknowledgement of DJ's arrival. That made the baby shower especially precious to me. In fact, I have every card that was given to us that day saved in my cedar chest!

The days were quite full, but there were times I heard God's voice in the night, when everything was still and quiet, when I couldn't sleep, when I lay there wondering what would happen to our DJ and to our family. Tears would silently roll down my cheeks. I worried about Derek and David. How would they take it if DJ died? They were all three little doorsteps—so close. My mind would race to the "what if" and the "if only."

I had to learn to literally take every one of my thoughts and compare them to what the Bible says and ask myself, "Is this right? Is it correct? Is this concern and fear in accordance with His Word?" I had to trust Him for the day.

Philippians 4 says, *"Think on these things brethren, whatever is true, right, good, lovely, excellent and praiseworthy and the God of peace will rule your heart and mind in Christ Jesus."*

I had to purposefully set my mind on the truth—but what *was* the truth? I had to distinguish what was true about our situation. I frequently asked myself questions to bring myself to the truth, "Did I believe God made DJ? Did I believe God knew the situation we were in? Did He know and did He care?" I knew that I had to seek the answers in scripture. That is the one source of truth that never changes:

> Psalm 139 says, *God skillfully wove together my son in my womb and that He was intimately acquainted with DJ. It says God's eyes saw DJ's unformed substance and all of DJ's days appointed for him were written in God's book.*

I realized the truth was I did believe that God formed DJ. He made my son. God wasn't surprised when DJ was born. He knew all about his little heart. God knew and called DJ by name before he was born.

I had to wrestle with this truth, because I thought, "Well, if You knew, You could have fixed his heart." I know it actually is true that He could have fixed it—but I also know God said this world is no longer perfect. He said He would be my strength in times of trouble. He said He would direct my steps. He would be strong when I was weak. He said I could rely on Him, trust in Him and that He somehow would cause His goodness, majesty and glory to shine through, in spite of the condition of DJ's heart.

God showed Dan and me through countless ways that He is Faithful. I just needed reminders along the way. When we recounted the journey, we remembered that God knew I shouldn't have anesthesia at the delivery. He knew Dr. Warren would be there and capable of getting DJ ready for swift transport. He knew the plans He had for DJ and for us.

So I could choose to worry—but it wouldn't add one day to DJ's life. All of my worrying couldn't save Derek or David from the probable loss of their brother—but God even knew this. He chose for Derek to be the oldest and David the youngest. God chose their days, as well as DJ's, and so, for me, it came down to God's question: "Do you trust Me?"

I would cry out, "Yes, God, I trust you!"

His whisper of reply was "Then rest in Me."

I would respond like a child running into her Father's arms after she had been scared or hurt. God comforted me and taught me many things during this time.

✧ CHAPTER THREE
IN THE GARDEN

"Yes even though I walk through the valley of the shadow of death I shall fear no evil for Thy rod and Thy staff do comfort me" King David—Psalm 23

Then came a day that I will never forget: DJ was scheduled for a routine checkup at the heart center but, first, I stopped at a friend's house to pray. Nelda, who has since passed away, was very dear to me and just being with her comforted me. I was looking forward to seeing DJ's cardiologist, because he was always direct with me and never made me feel like I couldn't understand what was going on. Nor did he discourage me from being involved with my son's care. To me, he was like a big teddy bear and DJ liked him very much.

This particular visit didn't go as planned but, once again, I saw the hand of God. It was supposed to be a "routine" checkup but, in the waiting area, DJ began to cry. I looked at him and literally saw him turn blue. I picked him up and rushed to the back toward the doctor. He took one look at DJ and told me to take him next door to Egleston to admissions, where he would meet us.

Within an hour and a half, DJ was having open-heart surgery! The doctor, whom I trusted completely, told me point blank, "Linda, I don't believe he'll survive this. We don't have a choice, though."

I felt panicked. Making the decision to permit the surgery was wrenching, but I believed there was truly no other choice. He would die without immediate intervention. My husband, who was traveling a lot at that time for work, was out of the state and couldn't be with us. I felt horribly alone and terrified, and all I could do was pray.

20

I rushed outside to the courtyard of the hospital to escape the noise and lights and confusion inside and sat on a bench, in the rain, sobbing. I pleaded with God to save my little boy. And truly—audibly—I heard the crystal clear voice of my Lord asking the now-familiar question, "Linda, do you trust Me?"

In my depths, my first instinct was to feel nearly offended.

In anguish, I thought, "Seriously? Lord, You know I have trusted You every step of the way of this entire, heartbreaking journey. I have trusted You, time and again. And I trust You now, Lord!"

And then it struck me like a stab to my heart. The question He was asking me to hear was, "Linda, do you trust Me? Do you trust that I love you and that I love DJ and that what happens will be out of My pure love for him? Do you trust Me—*even if I bring DJ home?*"

If I had been standing, the realization would have knocked me off my feet. The horror of the stark possibility of losing DJ—now, this very day, as I sat here desperately alone, helpless to rescue my son—flooded through me.

Panicked, I cried out, "Please, no Lord! Please! You know I will die, too. I can't lose my baby. And what about Dan? He is in the air right now? He's not even here! How will he ever deal with this and the boys? Oh Father, You know it's too much to ask. Please Father, please not that . . . "

My heavenly Father's voice was perfectly clear, cutting through all the clamor of sobs and rain and pleadings.

"Linda, do you trust Me?"

I stopped crying and asked myself," Well do I? Do I really trust You? *Do I?*"

Emotion flooded through my soul as I wrestled in the garden with everything I was facing: DJ's desperate condition as he was laid open on the surgical table, my husband being far away, my boys who adored their brother, me feeling the most alone of my entire life.

In sudden clarity, I realized, "Father, You know exactly what I'm feeling and what will be. You were here, in the garden, with Jesus as He wrestled with what He would face. You know what it's like to lose a son! You felt such sheer love for me that You sent Your own Son to the cross to die, so that I could be rescued. Jesus trusted You, too, and gave Himself out of whole love for me."

I remembered in that moment that God had a perfect reason for the death of His Son. It was a reason bigger than anyone could understand at the time. Even Jesus' closest friends, His disciples, couldn't understand why He had to die. When Jesus told them what was coming, they responded, "No, Lord!"

But Jesus submitted to the will of the Father and God accomplished His good and perfect will. And it was *GOOD*. Jesus made a way when there was no way. His trust in the Father showed me that I really could also trust. Jesus' sacrifice is why I could cry out, "Yes, Lord! Yes, I trust You. Yes, even if You bring him home—I trust You! You, alone, know what Your purpose is for DJ. I don't know. All I do know is that You are God. You see it all. You know it all. You are great and trustworthy in all Your ways. Yes, I trust You!"

It was settled and I never again questioned God in this. Please understand—this was *my* journey with the Lord. Everyone has their own journey and the Father knows you completely so, if you are struggling at this point, it's OK. The Father knows and He loves you. He will help you through your journey. In fact, He loves when we run to Him with our hurts and our questions. He is your very-present help in time of need. He knows you by name, because He is your maker. He loves you so!

Dan came straight to the hospital from the airport and, by this time, DJ was in CICU. He was very swollen from use of the heart-and-lung bypass. Dr. Kanter, his heart surgeon, explained that they had to leave DJ's chest open for the first 24 hours, because of the swelling. He had also received a transfusion, so his little body was really fighting to recover. We walked into the room and saw him with tubes, monitors and his little chest "packed." They had also placed a protective covering over his chest. They talked about the fact that they had implanted a temporary pacemaker, just to be sure his heart didn't go into an irregular rhythm. What an awful sight to behold. At those moments, I just wanted to take all his pain and suffering from him. It seemed like the worst of a nightmare for us but, for our son, it was unimaginable. Our precious little boy lay open, so swollen we could hardly recognize him. The Doctor said DJ actually did very well in surgery, but recovery would tell us how successful the surgical procedure was.

He made it through this operation and recuperation. In fact, DJ was recovering so well that he was moved to the floor after just a few days. Then, in just a few more days, he was up and around. Isn't that amazing? We were home sooner then we could have imagined.

The pain, anguish and heartache of seeing someone you love endure such extreme conditions is emotionally exhausting. However, the determination to see them pull through—for us to witness this little boy overcoming incredible odds, time and again—was amazing. Dan and I prayed and prayed and then we prayed more. We held fast to God's promises of strength and peace and His great love for us and for our DJ. I tried at times to comprehend all that was happening, but it was just too much. I had to repeatedly say, "Lord, please take this heaviness, this burden for my son from me. I cannot carry it. I feel as though I can't function, I can't go on." He was always faithful to bring me a deep abiding sense of peace. This, at times, was a daily giving, sometimes two or three times a day.

There were, of course, so many dear children all around us. It didn't take long to bond with them. It was during that hospital stay that I wrote a song (my disclaimer here is that I am not a song writer) to the sweet, precious little babies who had been abandoned in the hospital, because of their heart disease or affliction. I was rocking a little girl named Meagan. During this time, a song began to form in my heart. As I was humming, these words came to me as a promise to her and all the little ones:

Lost little babies, babies of His, your mama's not here tonight but, believe me He is. She's not here to hold you or kiss your sweet cheek; she's not here to rock you or sing you to sleep.

But rest little babies, babies of His, He's here to hold you and rock you to sleep.

Goodnight, little babies; now drift off to sleep, your mama's not here but believe me He is. He'll never leave you; He's always near by, so rest, little babies; rest in His arms, precious babies, once lost but now found.

Babies—sweet babies, babies of His—your mama's not here tonight but, believe me, He is.

I love you little Miss Meagan.

One afternoon in December of 1994, I was standing at my kitchen sink, doing dishes. The sun was shining and all was well. DJ was sitting on the stool at the breakfast bar, playing with play dough right in front of me. He loved to make all kinds of animals and cars and such and I loved to watch him. Suddenly, I realized he had tears coming down his face. I was surprised because, as far as I knew, there was nothing wrong. DJ had become pretty tough for a 4 year old. He really only cried when it was an issue of the heart.

I asked him, "Deej, why are you crying, baby?"

What he said took my breath away.

"Oh Mommy, I'm gonna miss you and Daddy."

My mind whirling, I replied, "DJ, you're not going anywhere and Mommy and Daddy aren't going anywhere."

I knew that the surgery, the Fontan, for which we had been waiting since DJ was born, was only a few weeks away. I scooped him up in my arms and carried him to his room. Together, we lay on his bed as we so often did when we wanted to talk or pray or daydream together.

"Yes, Mommy, Jesus told me I am coming to live with Him," he said, in a matter-of-fact way.

DJ didn't sound scared—just sad—but I lost it. I clung to him so tightly. We were crying together when, at that moment, Dan and Derek came bounding into the house, returning from an errand. When Dan saw us, he of course became very concerned and asked what was going on. When I told him, he didn't skip a beat. He just scooped DJ up and held him high over his head in the air and, with a big smile, said, "Don't worry, buddy. You're here right now!"

It was over for DJ but, just as Jesus' mother, Mary, had pondered these things in her heart, so did I. Was the Lord telling me about the outcome of the next surgery? Was he preparing me? My heart was heavy.

The weeks leading up to the surgery were very difficult. It helped having Christmas and New Years to celebrate. The holidays are so wonderful when spent with children. Everything is a delight to them. We decorated the tree and the boys' bedrooms were lit up with lights and sparkling decorations. The boys always made fine dance partners—we swirled and twirled throughout the house to the Christmas music. I can still hear them laughing with delight! Abby, our snow-white puppy dog, was ever the source of enjoyment, sweet and playful. She scurried about the house barking and wagging her tail as though she was dancing right along with us!

We could see how DJ was struggling physically. He was such a determined fellow that, when he began to say, "I can't make it" on a short walk, we knew we really had no choice—DJ needed the surgery. We always had medicines and pumps, so they were a constant reminder of the need for the Fontan. DJ was tall and had shiny, light-brown hair. He was quick witted and a little prankster. Derek, DJ and Dave were such happy little guys. Even though the surgery loomed ahead like a dark cloud, we were rejoicing in the moment. We had to choose to live each day to its fullest, embracing life. We played and laughed, we prayed, we sang and we cried. We loved every moment of every day.

In January of 1995, DJ was scheduled to have his big surgery. We knew it was necessary, because our little guy now had to be carried everywhere. He was increasingly tired and it showed. He was nearly 5 years old and he wanted to run and play hard, just like his brothers and friends. His little button nose that crinkled up when he laughed was now almost always slightly blue. His fingers and toes started to enlarge at the ends, because they couldn't get enough oxygenated blood. They, too, were bluish in color. I remember lying down with DJ at night, staring into his big brown eyes until he fell asleep.

I would stay there, drinking in every thing about him, his breath on my cheek, the scent of his hair filling my air. He was so beautiful. His hair with swirls of curls. His mouth was a perfect little bow. He had long eyelashes and soft skin.

I would pray, "Lord help us. Strengthen us. Bless my sweet little boy, Father." Many nights, I fell asleep in DJ's bed, holding his hand, relishing every minute God gave us.

Dan and I prayed and prayed. We prayed for healing, for direction, for strength. We prayed for our boys and we prayed for our marriage. We knew as much as we loved each other, we were vulnerable just like every other couple facing these challenges. We prayed for family and friends who were walking this journey right along with us. DJ meant a great deal to so many people. All we could do was walk in God's strength and power, trusting He was leading us on the right path. We had no wisdom or strength of our own.

DJ had the surgery, as scheduled, January 10, 1995 and, at first, we thought it was a success—but a few days later, we saw him start to decline. He once again had chest tubes and was on a type of medication drip that could only be administered in CICU. His little body looked more fragile than ever. He was pale with dark circles, a look of constant pain on his face. He barely spoke, except that he would whisper to me. I could see being isolated in this glass room was affecting him, so I asked if he could be moved to the regular floor, where he knew the nurses and the atmosphere was not so grim. They had no real answers for us. The pain medication was not enough for him and they felt that, if they took him off of the drip, his heart would not last long. We stayed in CICU for two weeks. Thankfully, Dr. Ravielle made arrangements for a cot to be brought into DJ's isolation room, so I could sleep with him. That was such a relief—DJ didn't want me to leave him and I had no desire to be anywhere but by his side.

He hated being there. After three weeks, he started to show signs of emotionally shutting down. He stopped looking at people, which was not like DJ, but he was in constant pain. It hurt him to breathe, to move. There is only so much a person can take. He was so little and endured so much. We prayed and prayed for a chance to bring him home. Is there anything more difficult than watching helplessly as someone we love suffers? Yet we knew, even in the suffering, God was there. He was with us and He was with DJ. He never left us.

By February, there was nothing left medically to do for DJ. His heart was giving out. It had worked longer than anyone had expected. He was released for a short time on February 14th but, within just a few days, fluid started to build up around his heart again and we saw he was laboring in his breathing—so back to the hospital we went. I carried my son through the emergency entrance, where the Doctor on call met us. He asked me if I wanted to stay in the room, because he had to immediately put a chest tube in. I asked DJ if he wanted me to stay with him and he said yes. I told him what the doctor had to do. He was so incredibly brave. I stayed and held my boy, staring into his eyes, trying to give him strength, praying for him to be able to withstand this insanity. The doctor was so very kind. Poor DJ had had enough! I remember that Doctor well. He had a son DJ's age and it took everything in him not to cry right along with us. He was very kind to DJ.

In March, we saw him slipping away a little each day. The hospital, pain, tubes and medicines were all taking a toll on our little man. He was working so hard just to breathe. Dan and I had discussed years earlier that, if it ever came to this point, we wanted DJ to be home with us, in his own bed, surrounded by everything good and familiar.

Now the time had come.

His doctors held true to their promise and, on March 3rd—my birthday—my gift was bringing our son home at last, to begin our last precious days together on earth.

ꙮ CHAPTER FOUR
SAYING FAREWELL

But we do not want you to be uninformed, brethren, about those who are asleep, so that you do not grieve as do the rest who have no hope. (1 Thess. 4:13)

On the morning of March 13, 1995, everything seemed as normal as the previous 10 days. Our routine began the same as always—Dan was up getting ready for work as I was preparing medicines for DJ and getting Derek and David up and around. Of course, DJ could not walk; we carried him from room to room, wherever he wanted to go. He was very uncomfortable as fluid built up in his body and his heart slowed day by day.

Dan had to go to work, though he hated to leave us, but we had no idea how long DJ would be in this state. In fact, we were told it could be months. As we did every morning, we kissed goodbye and then he kissed the boys and prayed over us. As he walked out the door, he would say over and over, "I'll see you all when I get home—I love you" and, reluctantly, off he went to work.

After bringing DJ into the living room to lay on the couch, I sat with his head in my lap. I gently stroked his soft hair, making little curls and swirls between my fingers. Looking at every inch, measuring each breath, listening for every sound, completely in tune to his needs.

Suddenly, DJ whispered, "Oh Mommy, look! Look at them! Aren't they beautiful?!"

I didn't see anything and, puzzled, asked, "What, DJ? What do you see, baby?"

His eyes were aglow.

"Look, Mommy!" he urged, insistent. "They are sooo beautiful! See the angels, Mommy!"

Truly, this didn't shock me, since the presence of God was very evident to us during those days. We had an incredible sense of awe.

"Can you describe them to me, DJ?"

He said, "Oh. No, Mommy, but they are soo pretty!"

In my heart, I praised God for showing His beautiful, awesome servants to DJ. God is so thoughtful and kind and I was thankful that He let me be a witness to DJ's joy. I knew the Lord had let him see those angels for a reason. This, of course, ministered to me as well. I knew I felt the presence of the Lord in our house. How else could you explain this undeniable peace in the midst of a storm?

"OK, baby, just rest," I said, gently. Derek and David came in and out of the room throughout the morning, playing quietly. All was calm and peaceful. Derek would look into my eyes and I would tell him I loved him. He always smiled, but I knew he was aware that the situation had changed. Often, at bedtime when tucking the boys in, Derek would ask me if DJ was going to heaven. I could only answer the truth: I didn't know when but soon, yes, he would be going to heaven. Derek and Dave slept together many nights. Derek would read to Dave until both fell asleep. Derek was almost 6 and David was 3.

That day, the afternoon sunshine filtered through our tall living room window. It was luminous and warm. The promise of spring was right around the corner.

Around noon, DJ was growing very tired and he wanted to go back into bed, so he could sleep. He asked me to lay down with him and I was eager to savor every moment together that God gave us. DJ soon dozed.

After I checked his pump and oxygen, then measured out and pushed his afternoon medicines into his feeding tube, I rested on my cot right next to his bed. It was very peaceful and I drifted off to sleep for a few minutes.

Startled awake by a totally unfamiliar sound, I heard a soft, deep gurgle from DJ as he breathed. I listened very closely and thought the sound was from his chest. Somehow, I just knew this was a sign he would be leaving us soon. It didn't seem that he was struggling to breathe—but his lungs now had that unnerving crackling sound.

I knew I needed to get Dan home quickly. I called the hospice nurse and she confirmed my suspicions about the sound I had heard, so I calmly phoned Dan at work. I had felt an inner certainty that this day would be DJ's last on earth and, somehow, I felt secure in God's perfect will.

Dan was in a meeting, so I had the secretary interrupt it.

"Honey, I am pretty sure it's time. You need to come home, right away."

Oh how I hated making that phone call, but I knew Dan would want every minute he could have with his son and there was no way to know how quickly DJ would go. I was praying continually, but wasn't panicked at all. It felt as though the Lord was leading me by the hand.

Concerned about the boys and knowing they needed to say goodbye to each other, I called Derek to my side. I didn't think about what to say or how they would react—I felt this was of the Lord. Looking into his big, blue eyes and taking him by the hand, I asked Derek to come say goodbye to his brother, and then led him into DJ's room.

Derek climbed up on the bed next to his little brother, his best friend.

"Oh, God, help him to do this," I prayed, silently. "We need You right now."

Derek took DJ's hands and looked into his eyes and said, "DJ . . . I love you, DJ. Goodbye. I'm going to miss you."

Very softly, DJ responded, "I love you, too, Derek. You're my brother and I love you to the top of Heaven. I love you. Bye-bye, Derek."

As DJ slipped off to sleep once again, Derek cautiously gave his brother a kiss on the cheek and I walked him out of the bedroom. Derek was such a protector. It was just a part of who he was even at such a young age. He wanted to make it better for his brother. He wanted *me* to make it better and all I could do was help to walk him through this difficult good-bye.

I took Derek out on the back deck. He was crying, with big tears freely rolling down his cheeks.

"Mommy, is DJ going to Heaven now?" he asked, solemnly. "Is he going to be with Jesus?"

Hugging him, I answered, "Yes, baby, he is getting ready now. It will be soon."

Crying, Derek asked, "Why, Mommy? Why does Jesus have to take my brother? I don't want him to go! Why can't he stay here with us? We can take care of him."

I cried with Derek, holding him and wiping away his tears. Trying my best to explain, I said, "DJ's heart is just sick, Derek. There is nothing we can do to make it better. Your heart keeps you alive and DJ's heart isn't strong enough to keep beating anymore."

We had talked about DJ's heart many times before, so I wasn't telling him something new, but I wanted to remind him and try to help him understand that DJ wasn't scared to go. I reminded him of the angels and how DJ had told us he would be going to be with Jesus soon.

"You know Jesus loves DJ, Derek, and He is waiting for him so that, when DJ's heart stops beating and he takes his last breath here on earth, he will immediately be right there in Heaven with Jesus," I reassured him. "Don't worry. Jesus will take good care of your brother. It's not like sleeping, when you close your eyes and everything looks dark. No, it's like when you wake up in the morning and everything is bright and the sun is shining and you're excited, because you know today is a special day and you just can't wait!"

"Today is DJ's special day, because today DJ will be with Jesus," I said, squeezing him tightly. "Now I need to go and take care of your brother." I explained that Ms. Lorie was coming to get him and Dave until Aunt Kim and Uncle Randy got there. They would then go home with Kim and Randy and their cousins and spend the night with them. I explained that Daddy and I had to stay with DJ and take care of him. Derek seemed okay with leaving and I knew they would feel safe at Kim and Randy's home. I told him that we would see them the next day. I asked if he was ok and he said yes.

We hugged for a long time and I told him, "I love you so much!"

My heart ached for him. Derek was three months shy of 6—old enough to feel all the emotions of uncertainty and fear—and even, I believe, the desire to save his brother. I was keenly aware of my responsibility to my precious boys to tell them the truth, while setting their minds at ease as much as possible. I did the best I could but, even in this, I needed to trust the Lord to minister to them at this crucial time. No words seem sufficient. There are not enough hugs or promises to make it all better.

Next, I brought David into DJ's bedroom. David had just turned 3 that February. I could tell he knew something was wrong. He was hesitant as we walked into the room and his forehead was wrinkled up in a frown. Still very attached to me, Dave held on tightly as I told him that it was time to say goodbye to his brother. I gently set him down on the bed and he snuggled up to his big brother.

"Bye-bye, DJ," he said.

DJ replied, "I love you, Davey. I love you."

They kissed each other on the cheek and, once more, DJ fell asleep. I lifted David up into my arms, again, holding him near, praying God would minister to my sweet little one, who was too young to make sense of saying goodbye to his brother who was laying right there in his own bed. I didn't think Davey could comprehend DJ dying.

I did whisper in his ear that DJ was going to be with Jesus.

"Me, too?" David asked, knowing that, wherever DJ went, he always went "also."

Hugging him, I said, "No, baby, not this time."

When I called my friend to come and pick up the boys, I could hear her hesitation. She told me later that, as she walked down the street to pick up Derek and David, she was very nervous and didn't know what to expect.

"I walked in scared and nervous," she told me, "but, as soon as I walked into the house, an incredible sensation like a cool mist surrounded me. I became calm as I walked up the stairs and down the hallway toward DJ's room. Everything was so peaceful. I almost felt like I was in another dimension."

She said she could see the distress and fatigue on DJ's face, so she cautiously greeted him, and then left with Derek and David to wait for Aunt Kim and Uncle Randy to arrive to pick them up.

A friend, who was also our former pastor, arrived at the same time as Dan. God is so awesome! When I had called earlier to ask him to come to our house, his daughter had said, "Oh, Miss Linda, Daddy's on his way there, already!" God had sent him on his way to us—before I ever called!

The three of us took turns going in to be with DJ. He was very weak and uncomfortable. The hospice nurse arrived and verified that these were DJ's final hours. I asked her to leave, so we could be alone with him. She advised us not to give him anything to eat or drink, because he would not be able to digest it.

DJ was still aware of his surroundings, but would frequently slip in and out of sleep. Soon, Dan's sister Kim and her husband Randy arrived. Aunt Kim and Uncle Randy were dearly loved by all three of the boys. Aunt Kim loves to sing and DJ adored all of Aunt Kim's songs and stories. I can hear his little voice even now saying, "Aunt Kiiiim, one more!" so that Aunt Kim would obligingly say, "Okay, one more" to laughs and giggles on our visits there.

Now we were together at DJ's bedside. We prayed and Kim began to sing. It was a very solemn moment until, all of a sudden, DJ spoke up with an authoritative tone, "Aunt Kim, stop singing!" We all started to laugh and Kim said, "Okay, Deej, I'll be quiet."

Only a few months before, at Christmas, DJ had sat on their dining room table as our family gathered round to lay hands on DJ and pray for him. That memory is so clear in my mind, because DJ just sat there, drinking it in and seemed strengthened by the prayers.

DJ's strength was nearly gone now. When it was time for Randy and Kim to leave, DJ wanted to wave goodbye to his aunt, uncle and cousins, so we carefully held him up to the bedroom window to see them as they pulled out of the driveway to DJ waving good-bye.

Once they were gone, DJ seemed extremely uncomfortable. Although we had an air mattress with a sheep's skin under him, it hurt him to breathe. Each breath was very shallow. He hated the oxygen mask on his nose.

It was evening and everything was very quiet until, all of a sudden, DJ let out a tremendous roar! It was loud! Dan and I were shocked, but it made us laugh. We wondered what that was all about, but we were focused on making DJ as comfortable as possible. I asked DJ if he wanted to lay in our waterbed, since I thought the heat and softness might ease his discomfort a little. He said yes, so Dan and I moved him, with all of his equipment, to our bedroom. Dan gently laid his little boy down and DJ sighed with appreciation.

"I'm sooo thirsty," he said. "Please, Mommy, may I have my Sprite?"

Well, you had better believe that, if that's what my baby wanted, he was going to get it! I knew I had been told not to give him anything to drink, but I was also determined to give him anything I could. As far as we were concerned, if he had asked for a steak dinner, he would have gotten it!

His pleasure was an amazing sight to see. DJ sat up on a waterbed for that drink! He sipped it long and hard. He drank that entire cup of Sprite and then let out the longest "Aaahhh" you can imagine. A sheer look of satisfaction was on his face.

When I asked if he was tired, DJ said yes. I asked if he wanted Mommy and Daddy to lie down next to him and he smiled. His eyes, although still filled with discomfort, were also filled with love.

"Daddy," he instructed, patting to his left.

"Mommy," he continued, patting to his right.

Dan and I climbed into bed beside our son. DJ rolled over and put his leg and arm over Dan. Looking back, I don't know how it happened—it seems impossible—but we all three fell asleep.

As the clock struck midnight, I awoke and reached over to feel DJ's back. He was still breathing. My eyes were closed but, somewhere inside of me, I saw DJ rising up out of his body. It was as though Heaven opened and a hand reached down for him. DJ looked down at me, hesitantly, and, in my vision, I told him it was okay. He could go. He reached up, took hold of that hand and was gone.

Opening my eyes, I reached over and touched DJ's back. Indeed, he was gone. I woke Dan up and told him. Of course, Dan's first reaction was to check. He immediately began to cry. He cried so deeply and so sorrowfully that I understood the word "wail." DJ really looked like he was sleeping. He was so beautiful—but his eyes showed us our little boy was gone. It was so strange, because we were looking at him and yet he wasn't there.

A verse came to mind: *"Absent from the body, present with the Lord."*

And I knew it to be true.

On this day, DJ—our sweet, precious son—had gone to be with Jesus.

Eventhoughwehadknownthiswascoming,weweren't—couldn't possibly be—prepared for his leaving. He was gone and, in that moment, I can only describe this as a complete sense of loss, a sense of defeat, emptiness, darkness, pain unlike any other.

I can see clearly now that the entire time was filled with the touches of God's hand. I don't think, though, that there is a way to describe the deep aching that came with the realization of our son's death. It would take a long, long time to fully realize the loss. There was a shocking sense of disorientation. Every day, life had to go on, as we tried to understand how to get through, one heart-wrenching moment at a time.

The simple things seemed hardest—setting the table for four, instead of five, waking up with no medications to give, no feedings to prepare, no strict schedule. No doctors or drives to the heart center. No more surgeries. Would I ever see the hospital and staff again? This was difficult, to say the least. Emotions erupted at the most unexpected times.

Others also needed comforting. I had two boys who needed my care. How was life going to go on? It could never be the same. Derek's buddy, his little co-conspirator, was gone. David had been DJ's shadow. Everywhere DJ went, he would take Dave by the hand and said, "Davey wants to go, too."

Gone. He was *gone*.

We each had our own grief to experience. We all had to find a new way to "fit" as a family. It seemed to me that the world should have stopped. Everyone should have realized that one of the most amazing people in the world was not here, anymore.

But the world did go on. Time didn't stop. I felt like I was in a time warp. I would think of doing something—and then I would find out I had already done it. I had to force myself to carry on, but I felt inept. Nothing seemed quite "right" to me.

It has been several years since DJ went to be with the Lord. It is amazing to me that we can again laugh and play and live life to the fullest. It wasn't quickly this way, though. It has taken time. It has taken prayer. It has taken choice. It has been a journey.

I remember thinking, "Life will never be good, again. There will always be a part of me that will be dead." It almost felt as if that would somehow show DJ, and perhaps others, how much I missed him.

At times, I prayed, "Father, how can You expect me to go on? I can't. I won't." I did, though. God is faithful. His promises are sure and true.

Yes—and *Amen.*

🐾 CHAPTER FIVE
THE QUESTION OF DEATH

For if we live, we live for the Lord, or if we die, we die for the Lord; therefore whether we live or die, we are the Lord's. Romans 14:8

For a long, long time, when I awoke each morning, my heart plummeted with the fresh realization that DJ was not here. Sometimes I thought I heard the pump signaling the feeding bag was empty or I would think it's time for his medication. I had dreams that it was all a terrible mistake and, somehow, DJ was really still at the hospital—I just needed to go and get him. Those mornings only led to new heartbreak as I confronted the truth afresh.

Though I desperately tried to stop, I would replay in my mind the entire last three months—over and over. I went through the mental gymnastics of trying to backtrack, poring over whether there was anything I could have done or should have done differently to have changed the outcome. I knew it was futile, yet my mind seemed to be on autopilot. It renewed my grief full force. Sometimes I felt angry; sometimes, my heart hurt so incredibly deep I thought it might explode.

I then started to ponder the entire question of death. I realized that I did not understand why our God let death occur and felt that this understanding might bring a sense of peace . . . so I studied.

I had questions, many questions: Was I robbed? Did Satan steal my son's life away? Hadn't I been told that Satan is the one that comes to kill, rob and destroy? Had God forgotten us? If God could have saved my DJ, why didn't He?

Surely, my son shouldn't be dead. No, it had to all be a mistake.

I became confused about the spiritual nature of death. I was emotionally exhausted, sleep deprived and deeply grieving. It became apparent to me that I needed a review of what the Bible says about death, God and His faithfulness as our Father. I needed to be reminded of the truth about God, Satan, life and death. Feverishly, I studied and prayed and read and wrote.

In this chapter, I will attempt to share with you some of my notes and Bible studies put together as I walked—and often crawled—through this time. I would face a question, and ask God to show me truth and then journal what He showed me. Slowly, it all began to come together. I read respected authors and listened to teachings concerning life and death. I heard many different ideas about death and discovered that I had believed many misconceptions. I genuinely yearned to know what, in fact, God's Word had to say.

Some of the questions I needed answered were: Why does God allow death? Is God or Satan responsible for death? Is death punishment? Is death the ultimate end? Why did God first allow death?

I returned to the beginning: *Genesis.*

In order to understand why God allowed death, I had to understand Him and His creation.

In the first book of the Bible, we are introduced to Adam and Eve. They were created by God, in His image—to walk in companionship with Him. They didn't have to do anything to make God love them—He naturally, wholly loved them. They walked and talked in communion with Him in the Garden of Eden—how beautiful! Join me in this journey and picture this place called Eden, the perfect world God had created.

The vast spectacle of a finely tuned universe, our own lands and seas, and the abundant array of creatures on earth—these are all stunning, miraculous creations! How much greater must He have cherished the original two individuals whom He molded to oversee all that He had created? He made them to join Him in personal fellowship, His spectacular creation was not complete, until He formed them and breathed life into them!

Adam and Eve had all things wonderful—in abundance! The world God created for them was beautiful, with complete harmony between man, nature and beast, and food was plentiful. They were surrounded by the splendor of a perfect creation—and, best of all, God walked in the garden with them!

Still, God wanted people who would willingly love Him and choose to follow His wisdom and instruction. And so He permitted temptation to enter their lives. God didn't tempt Adam and Eve. However, He did not prevent them from making their own choice.

God wanted Adam and Eve to continue to live in perfection, in peace and joy. Remember, Adam and Eve only knew this kind of an existence and so He warned Adam not to eat of the Tree of Knowledge of Good and Evil—or he would surely die.

When I read this passage in the Bible, it was the first time I saw the word "die" in scripture. Our Father's heart was clear to me. He wanted Adam and Eve to *live and not die*. God's desire for them was that they would be able to withstand Satan's temptation to sin (disobey)—but they had to choose on their own. That is free will. Without them choosing to stay in relationship with God, their existence there would have been superficial and controlled.

God didn't permit Satan to force Eve to eat of the tree, either. Again, she had the privilege of free choice. Satan is called the Father of Lies, because that is what he is—a liar. He has always been a liar and he will always be a liar. He has one aim—and it is to deceive us about God. Satan wanted more than anything else for Adam and Eve to die and, knowing the consequence of her disobedience, lured her toward it.

She ate. Adam followed suit. Their choice crushed any possibility that their lives could go on unchanged. Indeed, everything changed.

Adam and Eve lost their intimate fellowship with God and could no longer walk, side by side. He could only be in that perfect communion with someone who was pure and without blame, sinless—holy as He is holy. Ungodliness is corruption. It cannot co-exist with Holiness. They had to leave Paradise, their home.

Consequence is painful.

I can imagine it this way: You live on the most beautiful, regal estate you could ever imagine. The fertile hills sprawl out before you. Each day, you stroll past that same ancient oak tree, with its sprawling branches and lush green leaves. The air is fresh and clean and just taking a breath is exhilarating. The crystal clear water of the sparkling stream beckons you. As you sit on grass that is velvety soft and smile at the lyrical beauty of songbirds fluttering all around you, a magnificent lion lumbers over to greet you and lies down by your side. You stretch out your legs, laying your head on his strong back and taking in the beauty of the heavens. Everywhere you look, there is a glorious abundance of color, rich and pleasant to the senses. You are surrounded by a plentiful variety of fruits, vegetables, nuts and berries. Life is utterly perfect. God the Father and Creator walks with you in close friendship, you walk and talk with Him and it seems He takes delight in just being with you. You are always surrounded by His glory, swirling around you as light clothes you and music lifts you to unspeakable joy. Your every need is met—fulfilled and content you know no other life!

Then you choose to ignore God's warning and you take the forbidden bite into heartbreaking knowledge—the knowledge of sin, pride and selfishness.

Suddenly, you are no longer are able to stay in the only home you have ever known. Angels or guardians with flaming swords guard the entrance so you cannot enter back in. Life as you knew it has forever ended. Everything has changed. Now you must work the earth, till, plant and harvest. The sun, once warm and inviting, now blazes down on you as you fight to get the earth to yield food. Thorns and thistles compete for space with your sparse vegetables.

Night brings the need for shelter. Hungry, fierce lions roar nearby and fear grips your heart. Childbirth introduces searing pain and the heartache that is a parent's companion to hunger.

This and so much more was the plight of those who first chose disobedience over trust, evil over innocence, death over life. Paradise was lost. Adam and Eve actually chose death!

But Satan did not win. God the Father had other plans.

It is true Adam and Eve did die spiritually the moment they tried to deceive God, because their fellowship with Him was broken. They would also die physically after living 930 years.

Obviously, this was not eternal life. They had children and grandchildren and generation followed generation.

When Satan lured Adam and Eve into disobedience, he was certain that they would die and he would claim their kingdom, the kingdom God created for mankind. Likewise, when the Prince of Peace came to bring redemption, Satan believed death on the cross would spell the certain end of Jesus the Son of God. Satan was rejoicing when the Son of God hung beaten and bruised on that cross, because he didn't know God's plan for all mankind.

On that terrible day, cries of agony and shouts of disbelief rang out as darkness came over the land. As Jesus physically died, an earthquake shook the ground. God had set aside His own divinity. Willingly, Jesus came to earth to rescue us and save us from the power and separation of sin and spiritual death.

Satan was sure He had defeated Jesus. Because he is not God, he could not know it was not, in fact, the end for Jesus.

Jesus conquered death! *Conquered death!* What an incredible victory!

How do I know Jesus conquered death?

The scripture has multiple eyewitness accounts. We know Jesus left the grave, just as it was prophesied. On the third day, He rose from the dead. Jesus then appeared to more than 500 people! He was not a ghost or spirit, but Jesus—our Prince and Savior. He ate and talked and walked with His disciples.

It brings much comfort to know that just as Jesus was brought back to life by the power of God, a believer literally steps from this world into the presence of Jesus—from life to life, so to speak. They are not dead. They live forever in the Kingdom of God.

So, although every man will physically die, those who have believed and trusted in Jesus Christ do live eternally. Jesus paid the price for all sin for all time so that we might have eternal life!

God limited the years of man's life, because of sin. Death was part of the consequence. It was also a result of God's mercy, since He would not permit them to live eternally in a sinful state. Indeed, God's perfect will was for both Adam and Eve to dwell with Him in the Garden of Eden and for them to have an incredible relationship with Him. Their detrimental choice changed the future for all. But, in His mercy, God provided a way for Adam and Eve to still have a relationship with Him—and He has provided a way for us, too.

Remember Jesus said you must be born again (become spiritually alive) to enter the kingdom of God—born of the Spirit!

Satan is still telling the same old lie he told Adam and Eve: "God doesn't love you. You don't need Him." When God shortened the span of man's life, it was because of the evil that increased with man's years. (Genesis 6:3). The word of God says the intent of man's heart is evil from his youth. (Genesis 8:21) Man gave away all God had given to him, power, glory, authority—Jesus, God in the flesh came as man to take it all back!

I don't like when people repeat themselves. However, it is so important to understand death was not God's original plan. We know that nothing surprised God. He didn't say, "Oh no, they made the wrong choice—now what?" He knew the choice would be made to disobey Him and He knew what it would take to restore the relationship—and He provided the way. The cost was the very life of His only Son.

My niece, Beth, once said, "It's like when you plan on having a baby. You know there will be times the child will disobey. They will even, perhaps, reject you at some point, but you don't say, 'Forget it—I won't have a child.' No, you adore your baby. You love them right through their disobedience."

There is, of course, a difference between physical death and spiritual death, although both came about because of original sin. *Physical death is not punishment for the believer.* The one who has a relationship with Jesus Christ is assured of eternal life—stepping from this world (physical) into the heavens (spiritual). When we say a person has gone "home," it is a true statement.

I want to show you some verses in Scripture that specifically speak of God's sovereignty over life and death: God used these to bring clarity when I became confused about whether or not Satan had stolen my son's life.

There is only one who has control over life and death and that is Almighty God.

> *For in Him we live and move and breathe and exist.* (Acts 17:28a)

> *Before I formed you in the womb I knew you and before you were born I consecrated you.* (Jeremiah 1:5a)

> King David authored this: *Thine eyes have seen my unformed substance; And in Thy book they were all written, the days that were ordained for me, when as yet there was not one of them.* (Psalm 139:16)

> *The Lord has established His throne in the heavens, and His sovereignty rules over all.* (Ps. 103:19)

Precious in the sight of the Lord is the death of His godly ones. (Ps. 116:15)

There is an appointed time for everything. And there is a time for every event under heaven, a time to give birth and a time to die. (Ecc. 3:1-2)

"I am the Alpha and the Omega," says the Lord God, "who is and was and is to come, the Almighty." (Rev 1:8)

Can you see who is clearly in control of life and death? God alone is sovereign. He is God—the Creator and Sustainer of all things.

Death is truly stepping into the presence of Almighty God, our Father and His Son Jesus Christ. This mortal body is a tent—a temporary dwelling place of our soul and spirit. From the time we are born, we begin to die. The Apostle Paul said, *"To live is Christ and to die is gain."* We all ultimately leave this earth and, for those who have trusted in Jesus Christ, we will step into His presence and forever be with our Lord.

When we accept Jesus Christ as our Lord and Savior, we are indwelt with God's Holy Spirit we become spiritually alive and one with God. Incredible! I wonder—really—can it get any better?

I know the answer is *YES!* Right now, we see only in part—but the day will come when all that is awaiting us will be revealed!

When I think of heaven, I think of DJ entering in . . . .

He is standing before Almighty God—the Holy One, the Ancient of days. There seems to be what looks like a rainbow, shining brilliantly from all around His throne. A crystal sea flows from the throne and he hears the magnificent sound of angels' wings, like the sound of mighty rushing waters. Then he sees, all around Him, angels and they are proclaiming, "Holy, Holy, Holy!"

Then One comes walking forward with His hand extended toward DJ. He is the Precious Son, The Alpha and Omega, Jesus Christ! He comes to DJ, and he knows who this is—He has seen Him before. His eyes look into DJ's and he is filled with complete awe, struck by such a profound love he cannot stand, but Jesus takes him by the hand and they are face to face. United forever!

You see, death is simply the entrance and Jesus the doorway.

Jesus said, *"I Am the Resurrection and the life."*

God has established His timetable for you and me and for our loved ones. I do not know why some are brought into His presence sooner and some later, but I do know that our God does not make mistakes. He is not taken by surprise. He is not overcome by any obstacle.

He established the seashore. He set the stars in place. He created every person and everything that ever existed in the world.

So, some of the questions had been answered. God provided death out of His great love. Though dying was necessary as consequence for their choice to abandon trust, God loved them and had a beautiful plan of redemption for them and us through Jesus. He provided a route to restore fellowship between God and man.

So, does God wholly love each of us—even though we must physically die?

YES! And again I say YES!

Again, I do not know why some people are ushered into God's presence before what we would say is a reasonable lifespan. I do know through some who have shared their experiences of losing loved ones with me that God had revealed to them that, if their loved one had lived or survived, they would have been in terrible pain or agony. We all want the precious people in our lives to be with us but, at some point, we must recognize they may have needed to go—to find relief, to find peace. If they want to go as our DJ did, God will allow them to come home. DJ had faith to believe it was time for him to leave and it was all right with him. He had peace.

When DJ first went to be with the Lord, I rehearsed these promises, these truths, very often. As I cried out in pain and grief, God's healing was already beginning. Although I didn't "feel" I could ever really be healed, I set my eyes, my heart and my mind on my Father. He must be the focus, because He holds everything in His hands. He has my days already marked out.

I must come to the place where I trust in my God for life—and for death. We must choose to sit at the feet of Jesus and let His love cover us like a warm blanket. Since He knows us intimately, He knows each heart and mind.

He also knows how to minister healing, deep within. Like the hyacinth in spring, before the snow melts, we step outside and feel the winter cold. We may smell the crispness of snow and see the lifeless trees, but there, beneath the snow, in the fertile soil, a process has begun. Life is springing forth and beauty is peeking through, ready to burst forth in vibrant color.

Healing takes place in our soul, buried down deep within. It is a process that is not always visible at first, but it's working its way up, little by little. Finally, one day, you will find you have uttered a strange sound—a laugh, which brings promise of lightness and joy.

You may not be there yet, but it is coming.

God promises He will be faithful to complete the good work in us. The emphasis is on God and He will bring it forth. The seed is hope and hope *never* dies. It may lay dormant for a while but, at just the right time, God will bring the smallest delight to show you a work has begun.

The Father knows you. He knows your pain, He knows your anger, and He knows your numbness and bitterness. I know it, too. You are not alone and you are not forgotten. He is with you always—constantly. Even when you don't feel that He is, indeed He is. That is His promise to you:

"I will never leave you or forsake you."

🎵 CHAPTER SIX
HEAVEN, THE WONDER
OF IT ALL!

For our citizenship is in Heaven, from which we eagerly await a savior, the Lord Jesus Christ. Philippians 3:20

Grasping God's view of life and death were necessary for me. As a natural progression, I went on to study about heaven. What follows are some of my notes in a very condensed version. I trust the nuggets I found are a blessing to you too! Most of my scripture references are from Revelation, Isaiah, 1 Thessalonians and Matthew, among others. I have not written each one out. However, there are now many books about heaven and, of course, your Bible is the real source for all insight! I am sharing with you what is sealed in my heart through years of reading and praying. I am not a Bible scholar, but I am a believer who studies the Word.

Heaven—the most beautiful place I have yet to see!

Learning about where my son is now and where he went when he passed from this world into the next was vitally important for my peace of mind. Understanding this and what the future would hold for him has brought me a deep sense of peace and even joy.

Heaven is glorious and wonderful but, of course, it seemed surreal. Coming to the conclusion that it is a real place helped me to look forward with anticipation to our reunion. I hope this chapter brings you peace, too, because clearly the Lord's desire is for us to know where we are going and where our loved ones are right now.

We certainly have an understanding of Heaven, because scripture is beautifully descriptive about it! Still, we can only "see" it through our earthly experience.

There have been times when I am worshipping and feel as though I am there. Maybe I am (just not fully, since my body is still here on earth)!

Have you ever had a dream that felt so real you actually had a physical or emotional response? It's possible to dream that you're at the beach running, talking and playing and wake up with a racing heartbeat—or tears on your cheeks. It felt *real*! Our bodies were still in bed—and yet we were not exactly all there.

So it is with trying to describe Heaven. It would be futile for me to try to portray it, since Heaven surely surpasses anything worldly words can describe.

My friend wrote a song that includes these lyrics: *"You tell me what my Jesus is like and I'll tell you what strawberries taste like."*

Isn't that great? I love the taste of strawberries, but saying they are "sweet" or "red" or "a fruit" just doesn't quite do it—you must experience it for yourself to understand what a strawberry tastes like!

Fortunately for us, we have many clues and some things to which we can definitely relate. There are also aspects that will be totally new to us.

As beautiful as this world is, it's only a foreshadow of what is to come!

Our God created all things and by Him all things are held together. He is the Creator! No one told God what to make or how to make it. Everything is God's. There is nothing in existence that God did not create! Mountains, rainbows, the atmosphere, stars, planets, water, rocks, flowers, molecules, atoms—it's all His handiwork.

So why, when we think of Heaven, do we think of Hollywood's version? Oh please—there is NO comparison!

Heaven . . . .

Let me try to capture some of the images suggested in scripture of our ultimate destination—but, remember, I am still on earth, too!

First, let's begin with what will *not* be there:

We know from the scriptures that, in Heaven, there is no suffering and no pain, no grieving, no heartache, no physical pain, no loss or separation, no feelings of inadequacy or incompetence, no abuse, no starvation, no evil, no sin.

Instead, we will be filled with such contentment, wholeness and joy! In fact, when we are in the presence of Jesus, it will be so glorious, beyond our ability to comprehend the love, mercy, power and awesome greatness of our God, that nothing on earth compares. When we fully realize the depth and width and height of His pure love for us, it may well take a thousand years just to comprehend that. But . . . . time is not the same there.

It can sometimes be confusing when we speak of Heaven. Indeed, I hear all kinds of statements and questions about Heaven. It's likely because our introduction to Heaven is usually from Hollywood and—let's face it—Hollywood may be a creative Mecca, but facts typically fall between the lines and Heaven is made to artificially fit a script.

I think it is really important to be able to separate fact from fiction, though, because story lines come and go. They are fantasy, but we have truth! We have a solid hope. Our destiny is not make-believe or a fairy tale.

So, how *do* I know it is real?

Well, the Word is filled with descriptions of Heaven: who is there, what is going on and what the future holds. It is not really a mystery. In fact, the mystery has been unfolded for us! However, there will definitely be surprises!

Here are some of the truths the Bible describes about our wonderful abode:

When a believer dies, he or she is instantly in Heaven. There is no waiting, no "holding" place, no separation from God—we are home! Soul and spirit have entered into the heavenly realm. Heaven, I believe, resonates with each of us as our ultimate destination.

I believe that, when we really let ourselves worship God and let go of earthly awareness, we do have a presence at the throne of God—even while here on earth. Scripture makes it clear that the throne is no longer off limits to us, but we can enter boldly into the holy place of God in prayer and worship.

Heaven, of course, is God's dwelling place. It is a "holy place," meaning a place set apart and consecrated for worship. We will worship, because our God will be there. It is where His throne is and, of course, Jesus' throne.

Angels are in Heaven—millions of angels. Beautiful, awesome, holy servants of God who are celebrating every time one of God's children comes into a relationship with the Father through the Son—and, of course, when one of us comes home!

When I think back to when I was a child, my impression of an angel was a fat, little naked baby cherub who was holding a harp and floating around on a cloud! A memory of Raphael's cherubs, I suppose, but it is so wrong!

Let me share what scripture describes:

Angels are created beings who are able to transcend time and space. They may be invisible or visible. They appear in different forms. They deliver messages from God to man. They help in time of need. They battle evil on our behalf. They are mighty. They are present on earth and present in heaven. They are worshipping the Father and the Lamb of God—Jesus, who is the Redeemer of the world!

When angels appear in Scripture, they are always awesome creatures. In fact, in many instances, men would fall down to worship them—but the angels will never accept worship. They will always point us to Christ Jesus! Angels are a part of God's creation and written accounts are throughout the Scriptures from Genesis through Revelation. They are real, powerful and glorious. They are God's creation and they perform many different roles.

There are also living creatures described in Revelation and Ezekiel that are splendidly created. But they are beyond description. There is simply nothing on earth to which we can compare them. This will just be one of many surprises that await us! They are awesome and holy creations of God.

Of course, Heaven has many, many saints (people who have trusted Jesus Christ as their Savior) who have gone before us, but they are not just kind of "floating around." They are very much alive and active, aware of all that is happening in Heaven, as well as earth. In fact, because they now have spiritual eyes and ears, can you imagine the wonders that they see—the colors, sights and sounds? They now understand the great plan of God and know the deep truths of everlasting life!

There's more . . . .

The New Jerusalem—the incredible, beautiful city of God—is in Heaven. Throughout the ages, we've heard storybook tales depicting a majestic city with "the good King"—but this city is real and it comes out of Heaven from God. The New Jerusalem will literally come down from heaven to rest on the new earth.

This will occur at the right time—at the end of all things, when evil has been eradicated and the earth has been refined by fire and made to be new. The Disciple John's intricate description of the

New Jerusalem has many of the same aspects of the Garden of Eden and the paradise garden, such as rivers and the Tree of Life.

The New Jerusalem is "pure gold, like clear glass" and its "brilliance like a very costly stone, as a stone of crystal-clear jasper." The street of the city is also made of "pure gold, like transparent glass." There is a river of the water of life that flows down the middle of the great street of the city from the throne of God. The Tree of Life grows in the middle of this street. Each tree bears twelve kinds of fruits, and yields its fruit every month.

According to John, "The leaves of the tree are for the healing of the nations. The New Jerusalem will be free of sin and we will be united with God and "His name will be on their foreheads."

"There will be no night or darkness and the inhabitants of the city will have no need of lamp nor light of the sun, for the Lord God gives them light, and they shall reign forever and ever."

In that new, transformative age, the earth will be perfect. The New Jerusalem will be the holy city forever. It will radiate, because it is made of jewels and gold, and the city gates are made of pearl and they will never be closed. All those who are believers will live on the New Earth and God will dwell among us.

The New Earth will have mountains and cities and there will be houses and animals, flowers and trees—beauty upon beauty! I believe there will be incredible creatures that will amaze us—and let's not forget the chariots of angels!

We will recognize and know each other—*really know each other!* God created us to love nature, to appreciate beauty and to explore and enjoy adventure. Oh, how I long for that place of perfection! We will never grow tired of our new home, we will not long for the things of old, and we will be satisfied completely!

> *For our citizenship is in Heaven, from which we eagerly await a savior, the Lord Jesus Christ.* (Philippians 3:20)

Dan and I know that DJ is in Heaven. He is with our Lord and Savior Jesus Christ and, because of our decision to trust Jesus Christ as our personal Savior, we know that we will be with DJ and our Lord forever. That is absolutely certain! With this fact in mind, we have never faced the question, "Where is our son now?"

However, we have also had relatives and friends pass away and there have been times when the loved ones they left behind have wrestled with that question of eternal destination.

I can only say this: God is faithful and He promises He will not lose one. We know God's word tells us that God loved us so much He sent His only begotten Son that whoever would believe in Him would have eternal life *(John 3:16)*. The word of God says He alone knows the heart of a man. In *John 5: 37,* Jesus said *"All that the Father gives Me shall come to Me, and the one who comes to Me I will certainly not cast out."*

There is no time reference in this passage—even on our deathbed, it is not too late to come to Jesus! We don't always know the whole story. I have heard many accounts of a mother or father learning years later that their son or daughter had prayed with a friend just before passing away. God knows and He does not give up! He created us to be in relationship with Him and is always revealing Himself to us.

I remember when my mother-in-law became gravely ill. She drew near to Jesus in the last years of her life. In her final moments on earth, when she was very near Heaven, she started calling out her husband's name. Dad was already there in Heaven, waiting for her, and it was lovely to know she saw him. She would reach up, as though taking someone's hand. It was truly amazing to see this woman, who would never do anything that seemed out of the ordinary or improper, say and do the things she was doing. But the truth is that this earth no longer mattered—she saw Heaven and wanted to go!

Mom uttered a word that we all were astonished to hear her say: Beth—la—hem. Mom didn't speak Hebrew, but she pronounced it perfectly! It means "city of bread!" I believe she saw the golden city and was astonished. She wanted entrance and, praise God, it wasn't long afterward that she entered in!

I dare say, though, that this should be a wake-up call to believers. Share the truth of Jesus unashamedly—you who believe have the Words of life!

So how did I deal with DJ's passing? I had to choose to believe God's Word, His promises, who He is and all that encompasses. It is through faith, my belief in Jesus and in His promises. Now, please understand—my faith is no different from yours. It is given by God, in order for us to believe. My God tells me I have a future, so I keep looking to the future! God says, "*I have given you a hope and a future.*"

I know it is hard to accept when you don't see a future, but He does have a future for you and for me. We must choose to take hold of God's promises. Read them, meditate on them and ask God to help you to make these promises your own. God reveals so much to us in His word, because He wants us to understand that life is so much more than what it seems. Life is eternal. We have really just begun our journey, but we must *believe!*

✒ CHAPTER SEVEN
HEAVEN CHANGES OUR PERSPECTIVE

"Father, help me not to dwell on the things of the past that I cannot change, but help me to reach out to the future that You have for me. I will press through, because I know You have a reward for me at the end. I am called by You, through my Lord Jesus Christ, to look past today, because Jesus has a call and purpose for me." Taken from *Philippians 3:13*

When I read these promises from God's Word, I make them my own. I take a scripture and turn it into my prayer.

This scripture does not mean to forget the things of the past—that would be a mistake. Our past is part of what shapes our future. We learn from our past and grow through our experiences. Our past is part of the mold that makes us who we are and who we will become, if we constantly yield to Jesus with it. When I say not to dwell in the past, I mean not to live in the past. We must choose not to stay there, reliving those moments. We can almost hold ourselves emotionally hostage. Through the lens of scripture, remembering will become sweet, and not bitter. We must begin to believe there is a future—a future here on earth, as well as a heavenly future. If we know there is a heaven and that our loved ones are there and one day we will join them, then our perspective changes. We have not lost the ones we love. They are alive and one day we will be reunited. That certainly does change our viewpoint, but we must choose to keep the heavenly view. When we are grieving, we must not let our minds wander wherever it wants, but we must purposely think on the truths that will bring comfort to our souls.

It helps me to think of DJ's perspective now. He is one of the people who are described as the great cloud of witnesses that are cheering me on to my future and to good works. From DJ's view, I believe he would say, "Live life, Momma! Live to the fullest! Make each day count! Tell everyone about Jesus and what waits!"

I can just see his beautiful brown eyes twinkling like the stars of heaven!

> *Knowing, holding fast to the truth that God who raised The Lord Jesus will raise us also with Jesus and will present us with you, while we look not at the things, which are seen; for the things, which are seen, are temporal, but the things, which are not seen, are eternal. 2 Corinthians 4:14*

Remember the things that we see now are just shadows of what is to come. All things will be perfected one day and everything made brand new!

John 14:3, Jesus told the disciples, "*If I go and prepare a place for you, I will come again and receive you to Myself, that where I am there you may also be.*"

Jesus wants us to rest assured that He is coming back for us and, while He is away, He is preparing our new home! Isn't that fantastic?!

I believe God places in us a kind of perception of our heavenly home. After all, if God knit us together in the womb and called us by name before we were born, He saw our unformed substance. Somehow, deep inside, we know where we really belong.

I remember, as a child, lying down in the middle of a big field. The summer breeze carried my thoughts away to a place I thought must be like Heaven. The sky was such a deep blue, filled with the whitest, softest clouds—so peaceful, so beautiful and so big! Somehow, even as a youngster, I dreamed of Heaven.

When I became a Christian at the age of 27, songs of Heaven resonated deep within me. Truth will always stir my spirit and I began to get excited! I wrote this poem about Heaven after D.J. had passed away.

What is Heaven like, Lord? I fear I do not know, I dream of a beautiful, wondrous place where all will see you face to face! I dream of a castle rising high and of cities shining bright and majestic. Awestruck, I walk amazed, enjoyment overflowing. I hope for a place beyond my dreams, where angels will someday take me. I'll meet my Savior Jesus on a golden street. We will embrace. He will tenderly call my name, His eyes will captivate my heart, His smile fills me with delight. Then He will lead me by the hand and I will see him, my beautiful son, D.J. strong and bold. My soul longs for your arms wrapped around me, my spirit is filled with delight at the thought. Till then I wait, I hope and dream. Home, yes home, I know this place; it has been in my heart all along, beautiful and wondrous, home where I belong.

As I said previously, the night DJ passed away, I saw him leave his body and rise up. I knew God had taken him to heaven. Here are a few more encouraging truths from the Word of God. I also knew DJ had seen parts of heaven and he desired to go. His earthly tent was giving way to his glorious body—and DJ didn't want to wait, anymore. Jesus had told him he was going to live with Him and DJ desired that beautiful place with his glorious Savior.

As I read scripture, it seemed to me that heaven and paradise were often used interchangeably. My conclusion is that heaven and paradise are the same place. Here are a few scriptures to illustrate my point:

> Jesus said to the man hanging on the cross next to Him, *"Surely this day, you will be with Me in Paradise."* Luke 23:43

> *In another account, Jesus led the apostles out as far as Bethany, and He lifted up His hands and blessed them. While He was blessing them, He*

parted from them and was carried up into Heaven.
Luke 24:51,52

In the Apostle Paul's account of being taken up into the third heaven, he refers both to heaven and paradise as being where he was. 2 Cor. 12:2-4

Because Jesus said the man would go with Him to paradise, we know that Paradise is Heaven. When Jesus said *"surely,"* that is what He meant—absolutely, positively, for sure, THIS DAY, YOU WILL GO WITH ME TO PARADISE. It is where believers go immediately when they die. They are present with Jesus.

The word Paradise is translated "paradeisos" in the Greek, meaning a walled park or enclosed garden—an Eden, a place of happiness. In Hebrew, it is an orchard or forest, from the word "pardeca." As I said previously, I am not a scholar, but I think it is safe to draw the conclusion that paradise and heaven are the same place. Perhaps paradise (Eden) is in heaven. That makes sense to me, but the important part is that heaven is real.

Another amazing insight was something remarkable: the tree of life is mentioned in three places—Eden, Paradise and the New Jerusalem.

- The Tree of Life was in the Garden of Eden. *Genesis 3:24* Remember that Eden was not destroyed. God posted angels with flaming swords at the entrance!

- Tree of life is in the Paradise of God. *Rev. 2:7*

- The Tree of Life will be in the New Jerusalem on the earth. *Rev. 22:2*

So then, by tracing the Tree of Life, can we draw a conclusion? The New Jerusalem is also the Garden of Eden—or perhaps Eden is in the New Jerusalem? The two are linked together. It does make sense to me that Eden, the perfect Paradise, "a walled garden," would be in the New Jerusalem. We know it will be incredible, more beautiful than anything we have experienced here on earth. Think of the original Garden of Eden: Adam and Eve walked and talked with God. It was a plush garden. I think of Thomas Kincaid's paintings. He was called the painter of light. I think Eden is that way, filled with color and light.

Scripture says now we only see in part (not fully and completely), but then (in Heaven), we will experience it face to face—meaning nothing hidden, in plain sight. Have you ever seen a tree in full color in the autumn and just had to stop and drink it in? How about when the sky is a deep crystal blue, the sun is shining brightly and the trees are gently swaying in the summer breeze? Or a winter morning, when freshly fallen snow blankets the neighborhood, shining like a sea of diamonds in the sun? Oh my, I think Heaven, the New Jerusalem, Eden will be filled with those moments! When we walk around, I think all of our senses will be filled with delight as we breathe in the sweetest fragrances we have ever known. When we see something that delights us, I think every sense in us will be able to experience it. We are so gloriously made now—can we even begin to truly imagine a perfect place and a perfect body?!

Now that I have shared with you parts of my study on heaven, I would like to show you some truths I found about our bodies in heaven:

> 2 Corinthians 5:1-3 *For we know that if the earthly tent (some people call our earthly bodies our earth suit) which is our house is torn down (decays, ages and eventually dies), we have a building from God (compare a house to a building), a house not made with hands eternal in the heavens for indeed in this house we groan, longing to be clothed with our dwelling from Heaven, in as much as we, having put it on, will not be found naked.*

> We have some form of a body in Heaven, because we know the martyrs are clothed in white robes. John saw them. He didn't call them spirits—he

said "saints." They cried out to Jesus, asking how much longer it would be. They were conscious of what was going on and even speaking with Jesus. (Rev. 6: 9-11)

When John visited Heaven (the third heaven), He had some form of a physical body: He wrote down on a scroll, he held, he ate, he tasted, he saw, he spoke with others and asked questions and received answers.

> 1 Corinthians 15:44
> We are also told, *If there is a natural body, there is also a spiritual body.*

> 1 Corinthians 15:12-58 This passage is all about the resurrection (the raising of our bodies from the grave), starting with the resurrection of the Lord Jesus Christ and then the saints (believers in Christ).

> Luke 16:19-31 Jesus ascribes physical properties to the people who had died. Everyone was very aware of what was going on. The concern was for the rich man's relatives who were still alive.

We are assured that there will be a Resurrection.

The resurrection is the hope of all Christians. We believe that God raised Christ from the dead and His promise to us is that we will also be raised with Christ! Here is the definition of resurrection: to rise up, stand up, used of the dead called to new life, to rise again #1453 *Zodhiates Word Study New Testament*

Our bodies will be resurrected, according to God's word. It will happen instantly, in the twinkling of an eye. This will happen when Christ appears. It is called His second coming.

> "Behold I tell you a mystery; we will not all sleep, but we will all be changed, in a moment in the twinkling of an eye, at the last trumpet." 1 Corinthians 15:51

"For the trumpet will sound and the dead will be raised imperishable, and we will be changed."
Revelation 11:15

Wow! That is so exciting to me! It thrills my soul to know this truth and it is the very reason we do not have to live in despair when we experience loss. There is a promise from our Savior, Jesus—the Resurrection!

We know what it is to have a body, because we have one now. It is wonderful to hug, to hold hands, to touch and smell a flower. We know what it is like to savor wonderful food and sit down to a banquet with close friends and fellowship together. Paul says there is a spiritual body, raised imperishable, in glory, raised in power!

"But the dead will live; their bodies will rise. You who dwell in the dust, wake up and shout for joy . . . . the earth will give birth to her dead." Isaiah 26:19

"Beloved, we are God's children now; it does not yet appear what we shall be, but we know that when He appears we shall be like Him, for we shall see Him as He is". 1 John 3:2

"And just as we have borne the likeness of the earthly man, so shall we bear the likeness of the Man from Heaven". 1Corinthians 15:49

"No one can come to Me unless the Father who sent Me draws him; and I will raise him up on the last day. John 6:44

Not only will there be a resurrection but, when we are in Heaven, there will be rewards!

When we are in Heaven, we will receive rewards. We will know how each little act of kindness helped or changed someone's life on earth.

"For the Son of man is going to come in the glory of His Father with His angels, and will then repay every man according to his deeds." Matthew 12:36

"If any mans work which he has built on it remains, he will receive a reward." 1 Corinthians 3:14

"Now he who plants and he who waters are one; but each will receive his own reward according to his own labor." 1 Cor. 3:8

"For if I do this voluntarily, I have a reward." 1 Corinthians. 9:17a

"For we will all appear before the Judgment seat of Christ, so that each one may be recompensed for his deeds in the body, according to what he has done, whether good or bad." 2 Corinthians. 5:10

This will be a glorious time for the believer, as each act of kindness, forgiveness, love and unselfishness will be counted. You will receive your rewards!

Isn't it exciting that we will receive rewards?! It makes so much sense to me that, here on earth, rewards are a motivator, aren't they? Well, why do you think that is? It kind of makes me chuckle when man thinks, "I have an idea—something that will motivate people." Well, the reason it works is because it was God's idea and we are God's workmanship! These rewards, however, are eternal and they will be greatly esteemed and honored in Heaven, because Christ Himself will give us our rewards!

Can you imagine that? I think when I look full into the face of Christ Jesus my Lord and Savior, He will need to hold me up, because I will be so filled with love, appreciation and overcome with emotion that I don't think I could contain any more than that. Then, He will give me rewards!!! It's really way too much to take in, yet it will happen to each and every one of us who are believers. Look at some more of these promises:

> *"and I heard a voice from heaven, saying, "Write, Blessed are the dead who die in the Lord from now on!" "Yes", says the Spirit, so they may rest from their labors, for their deeds follow with them."* Revelation 14.13

> *"Do not store up for yourselves treasures on earth, where moth and rust destroys, and where thieves break in and steal. But store up for yourselves treasures in heaven, where neither rust nor moth destroys and where thieves do not break in and steal."* Matthew 6: 19-20

Treasures in heaven! Isn't that just incredible—but that's our God: awesome and incredible, generous and full of loving kindness!

I have wondered at times if those who went before us are aware of what is happening on earth. I believe I found the answer, but I leave it to you.

In the book of Revelation, John writes about the martyrs (Christians who were murdered for their faith in Jesus). It seems they know God has not yet brought Judgment on earth.

There is an account of the Prophet Samuel's return to earth, when God allowed King Saul's request from the witch of Endor to call Samuel back, because the king wanted insight in order to make decisions. The medium saw Samuel coming up out of the earth—she described him as an old man wrapped with a robe. Samuel knew Saul and what had happened, both before he died and afterward. Samuel was, to say the least, displeased that Saul had disturbed him. Not only did Samuel chastise the King, but told him that, because of his disobedience to God, Saul and his boys would die the very next day. *1Sam. 28:16-19*

Just as an aside, let's be clear: God forbids us dealing with witchcraft and sorcery. It is not His desire for us to consult with the dead. In fact, He says all who practice such things will be cut off from Him.

Perhaps the most powerful account in the Bible, other than Jesus' resurrected body, is the account of the transfiguration: Moses and Elijah, the prophets of old, appeared in glorious splendor, talking with Jesus about his departure, which He was about to bring to fulfillment at Jerusalem. They both knew the current time period and what was to come. They came to encourage Jesus.

> *"Therefore, since we have such a great crowd of witnesses surrounding us, let us also lay aside every encumbrance and the sin which so easily entangles us, and let us run with endurance the race that is set before us." Hebrews 12:1*

"The great crowd of witnesses" are those who have gone before us to Heaven, cheering us on, as though we were in an Olympic race! I love this image!

So, I do believe our loved ones have some knowledge of what is going on in our lives. However, I want to be clear that they are focused on Jesus, the King of Kings, and are already in glory. They are not pining away for us, because they are in the heavenly dimension—time is not the same as here on earth. I believe they see yesterday, today and tomorrow in the light of God's great plan and they are rejoicing!

There will be a New Earth.

This is really exciting! A new earth—perfect and made for us to live on forever!

Revelation 21 and 22 mention cities, mountains water, trees, people, houses, buildings and streets! Sound familiar? Of course, it is the earth—a pure, refined-through-the-fire earth! An earth we can recognize, enjoy and explore!

67

"Behold, I will create a new Heaven and a New Earth." Isaiah 65:17

"As the New Heaven and the New Earth endure before Me, declares the Lord, So will your name and descendants endure." Isaiah 66:22

"In keeping with His promise we are looking forward to a new Heaven and a new Earth, the home of righteousness." 2 Peter 3:13

"Then I saw a new Heaven and a New Earth, for the first heaven and the first earth had passed away." Revelation 21:1

Isaiah 60 describes the new earth: nations, ships, animals, peoples, treasures, rulers, animals.

I know that all of this may sound like it's just too much, too good to believe, but our God has a perfect plan of redemption. Remember in the Garden of Eden all was perfect—that was God's original intent. The day is coming that His plan for us, for heaven and earth, for our bodies and eternal life, will be evident to us, because we will see it. For now, we must believe by faith that God is not a liar, that He will fulfill all of His promises!

As for me, I daily thank Him for all He has promised and the many ways He has blessed me. I hold on as an anchor to these promises. We can believe Jesus as our God and King, because He actually was the first to be resurrected.

The main point is this will happen—all that has been written from Genesis to Revelation. While we give each other freedom to discuss, disagree or agree on different points, we believers ultimately are unanimous—all of it will take place!

Why did I feel it was so important to include this section about Heaven? I believe it is because, when we know the truth, we can have hope and see the future God has for us. This life is but a breath. Jesus said it is like a vapor—here today and gone tomorrow. Knowing that we are actually eternal beings and that believers have such an incredible future, this gives us hope—hope past what we can see, feel, hear and touch.

Faith believes—not in the unbelievable, but in the truth. Did you know there were 44 prophecies about Jesus that were completely fulfilled? These prophecies start in the book of Genesis and continue through the Old Testament books, such as Numbers, Isaiah, Psalms, Micah, Daniel, Jeremiah, Hosea, Malachi, Deuteronomy and Zechariah. These were prophecies spoken by men thousands of years before Christ was born, who didn't know each other and lived in different locations at different times.

The Bible has been proven to be historically accurate. The Bible has been used by the wisest men of history and has benefited us as a society. An example is Isaac Newton, who read and studied God's Word often. He read that God had put so many stars in the sky that they couldn't be counted. Well, in those days, they certainly could be counted—they were counted and charted. This truth drove Newton to develop a telescope of significant power, which is still used today to see beyond what had previously been seen by the eye. He knew what God said was true. He acted upon it, because he personally believed it to be true. That is faith!

2 Timothy 3:16 says, "All scripture is inspired by God. Men moved of the Holy Spirit spoke from God."

The Word of God is completely different from all other writings. It does not just contain words of God—it actually is the Word of God!

We can have faith and hope in God. He is Faithful, He is good and He has a perfect plan. This world has pain and hurt and disease and death, but what is to come is eternal, everlasting, and beautiful—more than we could ever really imagine!

I pray you have found peace in this—peace and perhaps even joy.

✑ CHAPTER EIGHT
DEALING WITH LOSS
THROUGH SUICIDE

I lost my son to illness borne of heart disease, but I'm well aware that many families are struggling to overcome the devastation that follows something equally wrenching—a loved one's suicide. Their heartbreak encompasses an entire realm of sadness beyond my own and I so want to offer comfort.

I want to be very clear at the outset that I am not speaking from the perspective of trying to prevent suicide. If you know someone who is dealing with this issue, please seek professional psychiatric and medical help immediately. I am not qualified to counsel you or your loved one at such a pivotal crossroads. I urge you to speak with your pastor as soon as possible! Also, there are many great resources online for information and I have posted a few at the end of this book.

Suicide is a controversial topic and we've all heard plenty of strong sentiments. Some in the Christian community view it as the unforgivable sin. At the very least, the secular world says it's thoughtless and selfish.

Rather than glancing at this tragedy superficially, let's go deeper and peer at the person, then see what God says in His Book.

Anyone who chooses self destruction obviously feels that it is the only way out. It is their way to escape suffering, pain and fear. I use these broad categories on purpose, because our perception of the cause is not really the issue here. In my opinion, those who ultimately ended their own lives did so because they were deceived.

They believed a lie.

I believe that lie was intentionally posed to them by Satan. But, theology aside, whatever they were facing became all encompassing and it blinded them to truth.

Let me pose an example: A man, who is a husband and father, finds out he has cancer. It is aggressive and has spread throughout his body. He thinks, "OK, I am dying, anyway. The treatment will cost way too much money. The burden on my wife and kids will be too much. I don't want them to see me suffering—so the answer is to take my own life."

Of course, this is flawed thinking. In reality, his wife and kids want every possible moment with him. They would fiercely fight for more time and would never choose money over his life. But, when someone is deeply troubled and it seems all encompassing, his or her ability to recognize reality is often distorted.

Emotions are deceiving, aren't they? Circumstances can—and do—change, yet we can make a life-ending choice that hinges on what is true or perceived in a particular moment.

It is wrong thinking, but it is very powerful!

By allowing our thoughts to spiral downward this way, we create our own prison. The deeper we sink, the more consuming our belief becomes. Eventually, it rules our choices and can lead to our own demise.

Indeed, I strongly believe that a person who died of suicide was so immersed in faulty thinking that they were not in right mind. They were incapable of hearing or seeing any other solution.

I know this was true when I tried to end my life.

When I was 26 years old, I was falsely accused of making an error at work and fired. In fact, the owner had told me that, if I refused to date his son, he would find a reason to fire me. I didn't believe him, but he did it. It didn't matter that I was a hard worker, skilled at my job and gave it 100 percent.

I had already been through so much hurt and pain in my life and was putting everything I knew into being a success at work. I was truly devastated. I convinced myself that it was a waste of time to try, anymore, because people didn't care about me. They just took and took and did whatever they wanted to get what they desired. I was at my rope's end—exhausted, fed up and saw no future for myself.

I didn't tell anyone my plan. I had decided to just end it all. So I purchased a big bottle of vodka and took every pill in my apartment.

I gulped down the vodka, while sitting on the floor of the living room in my apartment. I was alone. I eventually passed out. It was just before Christmas and I woke up two days later.

I had vomited all over and was so sick that I could barely move. There I lay—alone, sick and, in my mind, a failure—*again!*

I remember crying out to God, "Why won't you just let me die?!"

At the time, death meant sleep to me—rest. I was convinced that God hated me. I can honestly say that I didn't see another option when I tried to end my life. All that I was pursuing was peace. (Wow, I bought into that lie!) I wasn't thinking of anything or anyone else and believed death was my only answer.

So was my assessment true?

After all, I worked myself out of a welfare family and thought I had a level of success. Yet, after all that, I had been fired. Sure, it was unfair, but to me it was more than unfair. At that moment, I saw no future, no answers. All roads to a decent future felt closed to me.

Of course, I was wrong! In truth, I had my whole life to live. This one incident didn't define who I was, though I could not see that. It staggers me now to look back and see all that I would have missed if I had been successful in ending my own life. In fact, it was just one month later that I started a new job—two months after that, I met my future husband and received Jesus Christ as my Lord! My life is beautiful in ways that I could never have imagined! I have an adoring husband, three cherished sons, and am serving in a community that I love! I cannot fathom that I nearly missed all of that—because I could not see clearly.

It feels important to me to be candid about this, because I know people who have lost loved ones to suicide. Every one of them, whether mother, brother or friend, felt that they failed the person they cherished. They are haunted by their belief that they, personally, should have been able to prevent it from ever happening. They are consumed by grief and guilt.

To each of those survivors, I say this: Your loved one was not able to receive the help you wanted to give! They were blinded.

Typically, someone who has become so hyper-focused on what feels like an insurmountable problem will isolate and refuse to let anyone else near. It is impossible to know for certain what someone else is thinking, even when there is a recognizable personality shift toward darkness. Truly, once a person's mind is made up that suicide is a viable way out, it is incredibly difficult to help them see it is not the answer. Sometimes it is a split second decision with no real warning to friends and family members. That person hit a critical moment and, whether it was rage, grief, a sick mind or body, they believed in that instant that this moment was their entire life and there was only one answer. It is impossible to know what someone else is thinking—especially when it is such an extreme decision that happens so very quickly.

For those who have experienced loss because of suicide, there is the heart-wrenching pain of "Why?" but also "How could they?" and "If only I would have . . . " Second guessing one's own choices further isolates surviving family members and can destroy relationships. It will take time and it will take decision after decision, but you can emerge from this terrible pain of loss. You will begin to see life, again. You will be able to move forward, but you must forgive yourself and possibly someone else who you think may have been able to prevent that fatal decision. Forgiveness is a key to being able to heal. Remember, no one has control over another human being. You cannot force someone to think differently.

Jesus commanded that we forgive others as He has forgiven us. This is because when we choose not to forgive, we hold that person in prison—but we are chained to them.

You may ask, "How can I forgive?" Forgiveness is not a feeling. It is a decision—perhaps a daily decision—to admit that this person (or yourself) had no power to change the other person's decision. Release them and you will also be released.

Truly, my heart breaks for those families who are dealing with loss through suicide. Healing can and will come—God IS faithful and desires to see you whole, again.

Many are also confronting the horrific question, "If my loved one committed suicide, did they still go to Heaven?" There are many teachings and commentaries on this, but I am telling you from the Scriptures, there is nowhere that I see this is the unpardonable sin. There is only one unpardonable sin and that is not accepting, bowing the knee to Jesus Christ as Lord, while you are on this earth.

I feel no hesitation in my answer to their destination: Yes! In my understanding of the Word of God, if they accepted Jesus Christ as Lord and Savior, then Yes! *I believe they did go to Heaven.* I feel confident, because of the character, grace and mercy that I have personally come to know as attributes of our Father.

Tony Cooke's book, *Life After Death,* includes the account of Rev. Kenneth E. Hagin's mother, who became very sick with depression. She tried many times to take her own life. She was a Christian, but she was very depressed and believed it was her way out.

If believing a lie and sinning could forever separate you from the love of God, then we could never have been saved. God's Word says, "While we were yet sinners, Christ died for the ungodly."

Yes, I said "sinned" above, because taking your own life is most definitely a sin. Your life is a precious gift. God has a plan for your life and it is NEVER for you to end it yourself. Taking your life is murder—plain and simple. God's Word says we are not to commit murder and this stands. *However, murder is not an unforgivable sin.*

I will never attempt to sum up, in a chapter, the struggle of the mind and soul. There are so many levels to pain and depression that most of us will never completely understand.

But God knows. He truly does.

If a person has a personal relationship with Jesus, but falls into stark depression or irrational stretch and then, believing the lie or through sickness of the mind, dies of suicide, I fully believe they are with Jesus Christ in Heaven.

You may ask, "What are the consequences?"

While I don't believe the consequences are equated to punishment, I do think there will be consequences. Upon death comes the realization of truth—Salvation is indescribable—to be known and fully known, standing before Jesus Christ the Lamb of God! I believe you will then fully know what you have missed on earth by taking your life. Your life was meant to be a blessing. You have a purpose! God created you at just the right time and you were born to the right parents to give you the exact, unique DNA you have. No one can take your place—no one!

It will be clear then, when we are in Heaven, that we were deceived when we contemplated ending our own lives. We were taken captive by the enemy's lie and believed him, instead of God.

That is where God's great mercy and grace come in, once again! Jesus will wipe every tear from our faces. We are accepted by the Beloved. This is grace—so beautiful, so undeserved. This is *LOVE*.

Nothing can separate us from the love of God!

When I think of pain, emotional or physical, I can't help but think of God, who hears and sees and loves. He knows exactly where you are in your pain. There is nothing hidden from His sight!

Remember that God the Father sent His precious Son, Jesus Christ, to take the sin of the world upon Himself. He was betrayed, abandoned, tortured and crucified. He suffered a horrible death. Crucifixion was the most painful, horrible way to die—and the Father chose to let His Son do this, as payment for our sin.

He did this, because of LOVE—His great indescribable love for us!

He created us and desires to be in relationship with us. When sin came, we were separated from God, who is Holy and Righteous. There was a division—a separation from our Creator—and He had to make a way for us to be restored into holiness and righteousness. *He made Jesus, who knew no sin to become sin, so that we might become the righteousness of Christ.* (II Corinthians 5:21). God the Father watched as His precious, holy, righteous Son willingly laid down His life that we might have life!

So, the Father knows pain. He knows grief. He knows what you are suffering and He is able to bring healing to your broken heart.

One of His names in Scripture is Jehovah-Rapha: "The God who heals." One of the ways He heals us is by His Word: *"He sent His word and healed His people."* (Psalm 107:20) The Word of God is different than any other word. It is supernatural! God-breathed, God inspired. Because the word is TRUTH—it is LOVE—it is power and strength.

God's Word has the ability to open our understanding when we read it and hear it and live it! The Spirit of God leads us into

76

all truth. Praise God, His Word is called the balm (medicine) of Gilead!

He reveals faulty thinking and shows us the truth!

May our Lord Jesus Christ bless each of you and your families. I pray you are reminded to choose life for yourself. You honor the person who is gone by remembering them and living a life that is pleasing to God. You and your families are in my heart and prayers.

Resources for help in preventing suicide:

Please speak to your doctor and/or pastor.
Remember, if there is an immediate crisis, swiftly call 911!
http://peoplepreventsuicide.org/
http://www.metanoia.org/suicide/whattodo.htm

CHAPTER NINE
HELPING CHILDREN COPE WITH GRIEF

"Permit the children to come to Me; do not prevent them; for the kingdom of God belongs to such as these" Mark 10:14

Children are the best recorders of information—but the worst interpreters! Children want to please their parents, so they may say what they think you want them to say.

When it comes to death, I think we need to accept that we can't explain it all—and they can't comprehend it all. Even as adults, we have a difficult time understanding death. My advice, following sudden loss, is to give little bits of information to them at a time. They want clear-cut, direct answers, but they don't need to be overwhelmed by too much too soon.

Realize that grieving will be a process for them, too. You need time and so do they. Address the immediate: Children want to know how this affects them. They want to know if what happened to the person who died will happen to them or to you or Dad. (If it was a child who passed away, this is more likely.) You will need to repeat yourself because, as they digest the information, it will bring them to the next level of understanding.

Don't try to force an issue. When they are ready to ask, they will. Meanwhile, reassure them constantly of your love for them. Try your best to maintain as normal a routine as possible. That is their little world; it means safety and security to them. It is actually good for us, too. Do the "next thing!"

Let your children be children. Give them freedom to play, laugh and pretend. It is simply too much for them to be constantly focused on death. It isn't healthy and will not benefit them in the long run. You must let them be lively, even if it hurts you—and it will at first.

I purchased a book for Derek, called *Someone I Love Died*. In it, the boys wrote their memories of DJ and feelings about his death. It was a great tool and now serves as a memoir for later years.

You can use an empty journal. Try your own questions. If you have a picture of your child with the person who died, tape or glue the image to the inside, front cover. Obviously, you should only do this when they are ready.

As parents, we must be careful so that we don't influence our children by our grief—and vice versa. I prayed before, during and after talking to the boys about DJ. I didn't talk to them about my grief and feelings when they were talking to me about theirs. I acknowledged how they felt and reassured them it was OK to feel that way. I tried to answer questions and, sometimes, I just had to admit, "Son, I don't know why." I always tried to reassure them that, whatever they were feeling, it wouldn't stay that way forever.

I didn't hide my grief from the boys, but I didn't reveal the fact that I could cry all day—every day, for months—either. Children imitate. Sometimes, they would walk in the room and there I would be crying. I didn't hide my tears from them. I told them I was missing DJ. Usually, they would say, "Me, too" and we would hug or sometimes talk about things DJ had done or said. I tried to make sure it didn't last past 10 minutes. I would purposefully move on and transition to us doing something or going somewhere or focus on what they wanted to do.

At first, Derek and David slept together. After a couple of months, we got David to sleep in his own bed by moving them into the same room. They needed each other.

David shut down when DJ passed away. It was gradual. He stopped talking and wouldn't acknowledge DJ in a photo. Remember, he was only 3 years old, so all he knew was that DJ wasn't here, anymore. It was too much for his mind and emotions to deal with and he just shut down.

We did a lot of praying for Dave. Dan and I held him and told him we loved him. Finally, a year later, we were in the car, driving back from a store and the floodgates opened.

David blurted out, "My brother is gone! He died, Mommy. I want DJ back!"

I pulled over and climbed into the back seat with Dave. I held him and cried with him. We cried until we had nothing left. It was the beginning of healing for David.

Dave had so many fears that he never spoke until that following year. He eventually revealed that he believed he would die or Derek would die. He feared Daddy might not come back from one of his business trips.

We had to address each fear as it was exposed. Through prayer, God would show us how to explain each situation to Dave, in a way he could receive it. Others might not agree with this, but our experience in this area bears examining.

At 5, David could not remember his alphabet. No matter how hard we worked at it, he just couldn't do it. I also noticed he wasn't joining in with other children his age. He was very particular about taste and touch. I truly believe that DJ's passing held David at the 3-year-old mark, emotionally. In a sense, he was frozen.

We took David to be tested by a Christian psychologist, who said Dave's test results registered on the Aspbergers scale as slightly autistic. Dan and I wanted to help Dave in any way we could to move forward, but help was hard to find. Finally, we were referred to a neuro-developmentalist. She explained that the brain is plastic—always changing and developing. Pathways, she said, are laid down in our brains from the time we are babies. Every developmental stage puts down new pathways in our brains.

She told us she could work a developmental course for David to help him lay down pathways that he needed. One of the areas that Dave had skipped in his physical development was crawling—you see DJ was never strong enough to crawl, because of his heart surgeries. It caused his chest to hurt so, instead, he would "scoot" on his bottom until he was strong enough to walk. David copied his brother and skipped this stage. Well, crawling is very important to mental development. The motion and coordination of right-hand left-leg, left-hand right-leg lays down pathways of communication in the brain. Since David missed this stage, he and Derek did army crawls through an obstacle course every day. We had other physical exercises to do with him and he learned by flash cards.

We did see an incredible difference very rapidly. David stayed on "program" for one year and was catching up. We praised God! With prayer for David and emotional healing from our Lord, Dave is right where he should be now. He is an honorable, loving, smart, compassionate young man.

Dave is now 20 years old—a happy, handsome, broad-shouldered guy. He is still not ready to watch videos of DJ, but we talk about DJ, openly. Sometimes, it brings tears and, at other times, laughter.

David looks forward to being with DJ, someday, in Heaven. I think he has a good outlook on life and on death. A few years ago, Dave had a dream. He said it was really great, because he and DJ were sitting in a backyard, talking and laughing. They hugged each other and started walking up a hill. There, they met Jesus and continued walking. When they arrived at the top, he said he looked down on this beautiful city, shining and full of color, and he knew it was the New Jerusalem. He saw incredible houses, friends and loved ones. He said, "It was so great that you just can't believe how great it is!"

I would say that this boy has a hope and a future—a country not of this earth, but of what is to come!

Derek, on the other hand, was almost 6 when his brother passed away. He wanted to talk about what happened and where DJ was. He needed reassurance. He would ask, "Mommy, do you think DJ is sad in heaven? We were best buddies and I think he is lonely." He asked if DJ was still sick, if his heart hurt him, if he missed us, if he could see us. He had these and so many more questions.

I always tried to respond with truth and read to him from God's Word all about Heaven. One thing I particularly recall was telling him, "Derek, you know when you are playing with your friends—playing really hard, running and laughing and, all of a sudden, I call you home for dinner? You come in and say, 'But, Mommy, I just started playing.' Well, really you have been outside for hours and it's the same for DJ. He is having a great time in Heaven and no one in Heaven thinks about time."

He said, "But, Mommy, I miss him."

I just held him, saying, "I know, Derek. I know you do," until he let go.

Derek wanted pictures of DJ in his room. He wanted to stay connected to his brother and "see" him every day. He would talk to DJ as though he were there. This was tough because, while I wanted him to stay connected to DJ, I could see that it could easily be taken too far. I didn't want him to stay in a world that wasn't real. I wasn't as concerned, since he was only 6, as I would have been if he had been older. Kids who are 6 still believe there really is a Superman. Fantasy helps deal with issues that are difficult such as death.

I wanted to help Derek ease away from tying everything to his brother. I covered these boys in prayer, night and day. Sometimes, Dan would call from work, just for us to pray for the boys. We sought out activities that would involve Derek. We didn't want too much going on, but looked for something he could achieve and about which he could feel good. He started the AWANA program at church and met new friends there who didn't know DJ. Though he told them all about his brother, he didn't dwell on the subject with them. He played baseball and found some creative outlets like building with Legos and drawing pictures.

Derek was always a communicator, so we continued through the years to speak openly about DJ, death and separation. Derek had a hard time sleeping, unless he was physically exhausted. He did emerge though. Derek loved people and new places, so we tried to make sure we went on vacation—even when we didn't feel like it. I often had children over at our house doing some kind of activity.

Pouring myself into helping my boys also helped me to heal.

Dan and I talked about how important it was to celebrate the holidays. We talked about how we would acknowledge DJ's birthday and his "Home going." I believe this is key in helping your children—having a plan upon which you and your spouse agree ahead of time. I know it is difficult, but it is better to discuss it and agree. Then, you can lead the way for the children. We would always ask them to participate or let them come up with ideas to add to the activities.

We decided that, on Christmas Eve, we would talk about how we felt, how we missed DJ and how he had always been so excited about the presents and the tree. We let the boys talk about their memories. We told them it was OK to be happy and enjoy Christmas. After all, Christmas is all about celebrating Christ's birth. Can you imagine the celebration in Heaven?!

This wasn't always what I wanted to do. Especially for me, the second Christmas was quite difficult. But we did it. We made it through and we actually enjoyed seeing Derek and Dave open their presents. I remember making decorations that year, as we did every year until the boys were no longer willing. I wrestled with whether to make one for DJ. I decided against it—more because it hurt too much to think of him having always picked out what he wanted to make. Instead, I looked at the ones we had made together as a family. So precious! Every year, I still hang those sweet ornaments and treasure the memories.

We don't talk about DJ as much during holidays, anymore—not on purpose, anyway. Now, we still mention him, but it's a natural occurrence rather than planned. It has become part of who we are as a family and springs from happy memories. These days, I have plenty of pictures around the house of DJ smiling and of the boys when they were young. I didn't create a wall of "just DJ." I don't want Derek and Dave to feel they have to worship their brother. I remember Dan once saying to Derek, "DJ isn't special, because he died. He is special, because he lived—just like you are special, because you are alive and here, right now." I thought that was so wise of him.

Children are special and we can learn a lot from them. They don't know what is appropriate to say and what is not—so they just say it all. Let them. If they don't ask the questions, it will hang like a stone around their necks for years. Indeed, I know adults who are still trying to understand their feelings about losing someone as a child. I know it hurts and is uncomfortable, but you must think more of your children than yourself.

Ask God for wisdom and strength. He is there for you and your children!

CHAPTER TEN
A FATHER'S ACCOUNT

In 1989, I received a job transfer from Long Island, New York, to Georgia and I was pleased. It would provide us with a home we could afford and a cost-of-living index upon which a single-income family could survive. Still, we were alone, with no family or friends in the region. Our first son Derek was born one month after the move. Derek was a blonde-haired, blue-eyed wonder. From the moment I cradled him in my hands and kissed his forehead, he had me. Derek was such a delight that we decided to go for Number Two. Soon, Linda was pregnant with our second child. (Personally, I always expected to have three sons—and had even said so in my 12th-grade essay about my future goals *and* when I proposed to Linda.)

Derek was a model baby. Besides his voracious appetite and the ongoing battle with ear infections, he was very easy to parent. Now, Linda was in Newnan's Humana Hospital to deliver our second son and the air was filled with the energy and excitement of expecting our new bundle of joy. DJ came in a big hurry on July 30th, 1990—unlike Derek, who had worn out my poor wife with 72 hours of labor! The nurse and I wheeled Linda into the delivery room on the bed and the doctor walked in, put on a fresh glove and caught the baby's head. Then, in between contractions, he slipped on the second glove and DJ was in the world! It was that quick! After the standard post-birth procedures, off to our private room we went. The whole process—from leaving the house to nursing baby—took less than two hours, with no waiting and no complications. I couldn't be happier!
Everything went according to plan, just the way us systems engineers like it—precision execution and nothing out of the control limits.

I returned home, which was only five minutes from the hospital, to share the good news, make a few phone calls to get the communications chain going, check on Derek, and grab a few things Linda had requested for her expected overnight stay. When Linda called the house from the hospital, I wasn't surprised—she knew to remind her absent-minded professor about the items she had requested. But her worried tone threw me—and then the words any new Dad fears came through the phone: "Get back to the hospital; there's something wrong with the baby!"

My heart started racing a little, but I recalled the delivery—DJ had looked perfect, with 10 fingers and 10 toes. He had seemed the picture of health! Just as with our first son, I had received DJ from the nurse after the post-birth bath to inspect and bless him, before returning him to the comfort of his Mom. I held him close to feel his heartbeat, inspecting his little body for any imperfections, and kissing his face to feel his breath against my cheek. My initial perception was a healthy little fellow! I've never been an alarmist and have always thought or worked through issues with logical choices so, even in the face of this frightening news, I assured myself that this situation would turn out fine.

I returned immediately to the hospital, where our doctor, Jasmina Warren, was waiting for me in the room. Jasmina was more than our pediatrician. In the 13 months that we had known her, she had proven to be an extremely competent, highly educated and trusted council, upon whom Linda and I had relied in the absence of our closest relatives in New York. She had put us at ease with her cool demeanor and proper perspective on several occasions. But her typical, comforting smile was nowhere to be found. She was serious—*very* serious. In fact, I had never seen her like this. The atmosphere was tense.

My confidence was gone and the blood drained from my face. For the first time in my adult life, I was scared. Our carefree discussions of the past were gone—now, she was calculated and direct in her descriptions.

"Your son is very sick," she said, soberly. "He has a very serious heart defect—maybe more than one. We may need to life flight him to Egleston. It depends upon if I can stabilize his condition. I can't give you the specifics without more tests, but he is very sick and we need to act immediately."

While trying to understand the unfathomable, half of your mind doubts the severity of the situation, because your baby looks perfect on the outside and the other half is in an emotional panic, because a trusted authority on childcare is conveying the worst message ever. I tried to absorb every word, expecting to be involved in decision making. But there were no decisions—only action. I learned that, to my surprise, Dr. Warren was also a gifted surgeon. She specialized in Pediatrics because of her love of children, but she was much more than a practical mother with an advanced medical degree. With speed and precision, she performed a procedure that minimized trauma to the baby. Using the inch of umbilical cord still attached to the baby, she threaded ultra-fine leads and, within minutes, DJ was on intravenous fluids—without the use of a single needle. Medicines were administered and DJ's vitals stabilized. She had acted so quickly that a ground transport called Angel One was already en route and could be used, instead of the life flight that was detained by another emergency. DJ was ready for transport. This was the first of many providential events that would extend the frail life of my little man.

In nightmares where you are falling, there is a profound sense of everything being out of control—kind of a free fall toward impact. This sensation enveloped me as Jasmina laid out the next steps. My thoughts swept from Linda's weakened state and my desire to comfort her to my seemingly perfect son, who was hours from possible death. With Linda's assurance that she would be fine and urging me to do everything I could to preserve our son's life, I raced to Egleston.

I arrived at the hospital well before the ambulance, filled out the paperwork in lightning speed and provided the necessary insurance information. It was frustrating to be able to do so little, but at least I could be swift. When DJ arrived, they took him directly into surgery, where a balloon catheter was used to open his aorta.

The surgery was over quickly and we learned that DJ's life was out of immediate jeopardy. The invasive procedure bought us a precious couple of months to analyze his condition and plan for the next surgical procedure.

The discussion with the surgeon was short and to the point, as he explained the procedure that had been performed.

"He's a very fortunate little fellow," Dr. Kirk Kanter said. "If Dr. Warren hadn't prepped him so thoroughly for surgery, he may not have made it."

As my apprehension faded and DJ entered the cardiac intensive care unit (CICU), the reality of the past few hours hit me. I was looking at him and he still looked perfect, even with the leads in the umbilical cord. It was so hard to believe he had almost died. Later, I discovered that Kanter was the #1 surgeon in the United States for pediatric heart surgery; he was also the heart transplant surgeon for Emory University Hospital.

To my amazement, Linda was at Egleston within 24 hours. My wife is not the athletic type, but she is a person of determination and conviction. Still, the physical strain and trauma of natural childbirth would surely kill a man, so I was a little surprised when she called and insisted she was ready to go straight from her hospital to Egleston. She said that, with great reluctance and against better judgment, the doctors in Newnan had discharged her. My guess is she was adamant about exiting one way or another, so the doctors knew that, short of restraints and sedation, a mother's need to care for her child superseded standard release procedures. Regardless of any dangers or potential complications, Linda had decided she was fit to leave. Without consideration of pain or injury, she was convinced her baby needed her attention and that was all that mattered. This was the first of many instances when the depth of Linda's inner strength was revealed to me—strength beyond human endurance.

The days of tests that followed introduced us to the third member of our medical team. Dr. Ravielle was a Goliath of a man—tall, dark and physically imposing. His manner and approach were like Ferdinand the bull—a gentle giant, with a full black beard and eyes of true compassion. Children loved him and parents trusted him. Lo and behold, he was another compatriot of Dr. Warren! The triangle was complete and DJ's dream team of medical professionals was formed.

Dr. Ravielle began to describe our son's heart condition, explaining that DJ had multiple major heart defects, coarctation or narrowing of the aorta (this was just opened by the catheter lab) and transposition of the great arteries, double outlet right ventricle. He also had a hole between the two sides of the heart, which was a minor defect normal in newborns and one that typically closes a few months after birth. In DJ's case, this defect helped in saving his life at this point.

Dr. Ravielle went on to describe in great detail the structure of the heart, the function of each chamber and how blood flows. The great arteries that returned blood to DJ's heart were on the wrong sides of the heart. Therefore, oxygenated blood from the lungs was not getting out to the rest of the body. The little hole was the only thing allowing oxygen to reach his brain and other organs!

Hence, the second step was to widen the hole to allow the blood to mix and allow oxygenated blood to exit out to the body. For the time being, DJ was stable and we were able to bring him home for about a month, but we soon discovered he developed an additional complication: the sutures in his skull began to calcify. These sutures are the serpentine lines you see in x-rays of children's skulls. They are the growth plates that allow the skull to expand as the brain enlarges from normal growth. The doctors assured us DJ would make it through this third surgery. The procedure required a large incision, peeling back the scalp, cutting out a four-inch strip of bone, shaving the edges to create man-made sutures, putting the bone back in and sewing the scalp back together. That may seem too graphic, but I want to illustrate the gravity of the craniotomy procedure and its invasive nature.

Soon afterward, he had another emergency heart surgery. Linda says DJ had seven surgeries in all, but I lost count.

Unfortunately, we were back in the hospital the following month for another procedure on his heart. You see, the plan was to let DJ grow as big and strong as possible, until he would be able to have a major surgery called a Fontan to actually restructure his heart to work properly. I use that term loosely, because his heart would never function normally, but this was a surgery that had already found some success at the Mayo clinic in Minnesota, under Dr. Kanter's skillful hand.

At least, that was the plan.

The hours and then days after DJ's birth were so hectic that there was little time for emotion. Dads are meant to be the protectors and providers of our families, so getting emotional does not help crisis situations. We may be upset or fearful, but these feelings must sometimes be suppressed, so we can make good decisions, act effectively and take care of the business at hand. Our underlying motivation is love but, as it is said in Christian circles, love is an act—not an emotion.

The question becomes "How much can a man suppress—how many traumatic events, out-of-control situations and heartbreaking results can he weather before nothing else can be stuffed down?"

Soon, we were all home. What seemed like an eternity was only 12 weeks and now things would get back to normal. There was a regimen of medications for DJ and Linda quickly adjusted her schedule to accommodate it all, without discussion or grumbling of any kind. Linda accepted her role as domestic doctor, as if born to it. She had always researched our minor illnesses and successfully nursed me back to health. Her methods were generally the application of homeopathic prescriptions, but now she was confronted by a much more significant task than dealing with a big, childish husband with a cold or flu or otherwise healthy one year old. Our Derek was full of energy and smiles, but he did suffer with some allergies. Linda was determined Derek would have his needs met as well as get lots of love. She researched every medicine prescribed for DJ and Derek and scrutinized each purpose. Every dosage was exact and administered to the minute. Charts were posted and instructions given to all who entered our home in caring for our little DJ.

Linda loved to travel, but I was a homebody who liked consistency and a lack of excitement. The more rigid routine suited my personality. Trips to the store were well planned, excursions briefer and visitors screened for maladies of any kind, since a cold or flu bug around DJ meant a trip to the hospital for bronchitis, pneumonia or worse.

I went to work; I came home. Our carefree days gone, the serious days matured us into sober parents. We developed close relationships with a handful of couples from church.

Linda and I always looked forward to our Friday night Bible study, as each couple hosted and facilitated an assigned chapter. Our time there meant a night out, close to home, and Linda needed social interaction with adults. During the week, Linda would take the boys to the park, to get outside and have a change of surroundings. Our lifestyle had changed abruptly, but simple things became our entertainment as we settled into the new routine.

DJ was a strange little man. He had the best disposition and seldom complained, accepting oddities like the feeding tube in his nose as normal. He loved to laugh—and what a laugh! He had his mom's sense of humor and physical comedy tickled his funny bone. So his doting big brother and father were more than happy to comply, falling on the floor and bumping our heads—anything to make them laugh. He and Linda would sit together and crack up at our antics. She and I also loved to sing lullabies to the boys and dance around the house to upbeat music, with them in our arms.

Our house was filled with laughter, music and song and we were happy at home. It was our safe haven.

That had not been true in my own childhood. Both Linda and I grew up in tense—and sometimes violent—homes. My experience was much less dire than Linda's but, nonetheless, we had agreed early in our marriage that peace and serenity would prevail in our home. We had arguments—okay, sometimes verbal fights—but one of us would always come to our senses and apologize. We took seriously the passage in Ephesians 4 that says, *"Be angry and sin not; do not let not the sun go down on your anger."* You see, Linda and I based our marriage on a singular focus—Jesus Christ. Some people may think that is old fashioned, prudish or even downright archaic. But I can tell you, with total confidence and over 24 years of happy marriage as proof, it works! This one truth holds everything together.

Think about this: When you take your marriage vows, you say, "For better or for worse." Who created the institution of marriage between a man and a woman? The consummation of the marriage establishes a covenant relationship between husband and wife. Who created this concept of a covenant relationship? If you don't understand the concept of covenant, I can sum it up as this: You would lay down your life for that person and they are equally dedicated to you. It's not just about physical death—like taking a bullet for them. It's about every decision, every action, and every motive being for that other person. And, when you are in that right place, it is not burdensome.

Yes, it takes effort and hard work, and sometimes you mess up. But the benefit of love in your marriage, strength in your family and peace at home is worth the investment. If Linda and I had a disagreement, we would search the scriptures and find the answers together. We agreed that whatever the answer, we would both abide by it.

I'm telling you the answers—every last one of them—are in the Bible! Jesus Christ created this world and designed how it works—all the laws of physics, mathematics, chemistry and biology and all relationships. Look at the Ten Commandments—they are all about relationship. You cannot be successful in life without accepting and yielding to the Author of life. Linda and I were bonded together in Christ and we knew it was the only thing that could hold our marriage together through all the trials and tribulations.

Work is Work

Maintaining your work ethic, while caring for your family, is like the art of juggling. With some practice, you can keep all the balls, pins and even knives in the air. I was a dedicated employee and kept the proverbial shoulder to the grindstone. Up to this point, my career had been the focus of my life. In fact, Linda and I first met at Photocircuits' Long Island plant. The company was small enough that we knew each other's circle and established a common set of friends.

Before our transfer to Peachtree City, Georgia, was granted, my typical schedule included a week in New York, followed by a week in Georgia. This routine persisted during my nine years of employment—five years in New York and four years in Georgia.

I had written most of the systems that scheduled the factories, integrating the mainframe inventory and customer orders with manufacturing planning and real-time production tracking. Having a knack for programming, understanding numerically controlled machines and enjoying the puzzle of algorithms lent itself nicely to queuing theory and constraints applications.

I was a "golden boy" of technology and it was my ticket from poverty and a broken home of divorce to success. When we were confronted by DJ's medical issues, it was comforting to have solid medical insurance and even a familiar work haven where my role was well defined. But then I discovered that the corporate world sometimes introduces strife all its own—and those stresses have to be weathered and managed, regardless of what may be happening at home.

When Photocircuits sold off a division, only the facility and intellectual property was sold. As acquisitions typically go, the upper management was replaced. The new management had what they considered another "golden boy"—but of management, not technology. I was reassigned into his department. It was pretty much business as usual for about six months until, without verbal or written warning, I was notified of my six-month probation!

I took solace in all of Psalm 5, but particularly verses 9 and 10:

> [9] Not a word from their mouth can be trusted; their heart is filled with destruction. Their throat is an open grave; with their tongue they speak deceit. [10] Declare them guilty, O God! Let their intrigues be their downfall. Banish them for their many sins, for they have rebelled against you.

I know Christians are supposed to forgive and I did not do anything to undermine my supervisor's authority or cause him issues, but lies and deceit break loyalties. In fact, I worked fiercely for the next six months, cleared my name, wished everyone good tidings and took a new job with Scientific-Atlanta in 1994.

There are several critical life lessons I learned by going through this unpleasant experience. First, it is God who justifies and He is the Provider. You keep your nose clean, do a good job, give a full day's work for a full day's wages and let God take care of the rest. Worrying, fretting or trying to manipulate situations will chew you up and spit you out. It will destroy you and have a huge, negative impact on your home life. So don't hold grudges or hatred in your heart. Be free of malice and ill will. Spite and a thirst for revenge are like drinking poison and waiting for the other person to die.

Second, I learned that work is just that—work. Early in my career, an elderly gentleman gave me these words of advice: "Work never remembers and your family never forgets. You can get another job, but you can't get another family." Companies, especially in this day and age, come and go like vapor, but the family is eternal.

If you are self employed or a business owner, segregating work life from home life is nearly impossible, but try to compartmentalize for the sake of your family. Have the highest work ethic, don't leave things hanging, treat everyone with respect and go home with little to no baggage. If something is really bothering you, it's OK to talk to your wife about work stuff—but be an encourager to her more than a moaner about the hassles of work. Don't look to work for your fulfillment.

Solomon says in Ecclesiastes, *"There is nothing better for a man than to eat and drink and tell himself that his labor is good. This also I have seen that it is from the hand of God."* But he also states, *"He who loves money will not be satisfied with money, nor he who loves abundance with its income."*

Ecclesiastes starts and ends with, *"I have seen all the works which have been done under the sun, and behold, all is vanity and striving after wind."*

If it's not about the work or the money, what's life all about? It is about family and relationship—they have to come first. Your life is a drink offering for them. Pour your life into them, and expend yourself for them. Do this and God will refill your cup continually. The amusing adage, "He who has the most toys wins" is a lie from hell. *He whose wife and children know Christ and are destined for eternal life—they are the winners.* Now that's what life is *really* about.

Taking Care of Mom

DJ had his second heart surgery, when he was about 3 months old. The surgery required the separation of the rib cage and what is called the zipper, an incision from the bottom of the throat to the diaphragm. The procedure was absolutely necessary, but it left a scar that marked his internal defects externally. The perfection of his outward appearance was gone.

The surgery was successful and DJ responded well to the results—an improvement in blood flow through the heart. He was more active and stronger than ever but, by his first year, he was still not walking on his own. He excelled in using his walker to move around the house and was extremely mobile using the mechanized device. If he was without the walker, then he scooted himself around the house by sitting on his bottom and, using his legs and arms, would propel himself in the desired direction.

He seemed stronger than ever, but the two years of his life and constant, unwavering maintenance of his health had worn Linda thin. She needed a break and the opportunity came in the form of a weekend away. Linda loved studying the Bible and had become energized by Kay Arthur and the Precept Ministry Bible studies. When she asked if she could attend an upcoming three-day study on Timothy, I jumped at the chance to give her a reprieve. Using a vacation day to gain a long weekend, I took care of the boys for three days—*long* days. Keeping DJ's regimen of medicines was the most difficult task, but all three of us survived, and I had a glimpse of the constant vigilance required to maintain his health.

Linda returned absolutely rejuvenated by the experience. It was a minor sacrifice on my part when compared to the improvement in Linda's morale. I'd given her a tiny window of opportunity to catch her breath, contemplate the frailty of DJ's condition and mentally process the last two years of her persistent care giving. It wasn't much, but this short break was all Linda would allot herself to recharge her inner being, before returning to the indentured servitude of caring for a child with a chronic condition.

There were not many opportunities for Linda to get a break—just an occasional night out with the girls, typically Bible-study related. Her rests were few and far between, but I tried to gauge her needs the best I could and give her an hour here or a night there from the daily routine.

My brother in-law Randy was transferred to Cartersville, Georgia and so he and my sister Kim, with their four children, were now only 90 minutes from our house. Kim is one of those women I liken to my wife—a selfless and tireless nurturer. She believes there is no trial too big, no family difficulty too great that love, compassion and prayer cannot overcome. She was my spiritual mother—the person who introduced this wild, unbridled youth to Jesus Christ when I was only 15. Linda and Kim were swiftly becoming close friends and Linda's trust in my sister's love for DJ and his well-being grew past even my admiration for Kim's dedication to my spiritual walk.

Kim offered to take the boys for a weekend and learned the detailed schedule of doses. We had our first husband-and-wife "alone time" since DJ's birth. We were thrilled and went to a bed-and-breakfast in Helen, Georgia—for one whole night. Though we could have stayed longer, we looked at each other, smiled and headed straight back to Cartersville to see the boys. It wasn't remotely a lack of trust in Kim. We simply had a night of freedom and, in that clarifying moment, our purpose on the planet was made clear: Our children were our joy. We desired no escape. All we wanted in our lives was them and we hurried back to their presence. We couldn't help it. We loved everything about being together—our own little nuclear family—and nothing else was more important.

During DJ's surgeries, Linda literally lived at the hospital. I would come up on weekends with Derek or by myself, depending on the situation. Every visit was heartbreaking, but not just because of my son's condition. DJ had two loving parents—we were completely and absolutely dedicated to him and a big brother that always desired to spend time with him. Derek and DJ never tired of each other. What also brought us to tears were the dozens of babies and children that were alone, with only one or no parents in the cardiac wing. These little ones—some with less complex maladies than DJ's to very rare and extreme conditions—were isolated from the world and their parents had abandoned them.

I remember one little boy about 3 months old, born without eyes and a relatively minor heart condition. He was so precious and sweet. Linda and I rocked him for the nurses when DJ was sleeping in his crib. You could see every caress and hug fill his baby soul as he received our small gestures of love. He wasn't perfect, but he was a happy fellow with a pleasant disposition. He hardly ever cried and he desired loving parents.

Linda was in an environment where her son's health was marginal and surrounded with precious babies who were neglected by their birth parents and needed daily love. Nurses on this wing had the highest turnover—not because of attrition, but emotional bankruptcy. There were a couple of very special nurses who befriended Linda. They were very encouraging to us and we tried to encourage them as well.

We were living on a mid-level engineer's salary, but I tried to bring some flowers or a little treat to brighten Linda's day. I know how I felt being there for the day—I could not imagine how her heart felt, being there for weeks on end. I wasn't crazy about living like a single Dad, but Linda was in a much more difficult place and, as her husband and the father of Derek and now David, my support and encouragement was more than a responsibility—it was a God-given ministry.

How Much Can He Take

The next two years were absolutely insane. Yes, you should be scared, knowing this is coming from a guy whose life had already been turned upside down in under six months. New York to Atlanta is a short flight—unless you've just been informed your boy went in for a checkup and was rushed into emergency surgery! The hole enlarged by the balloon catheter had almost grown closed. When Linda brought DJ to the hospital for a scheduled appointment, on the way in the front door, he turned blue and went into heart failure. If he hadn't been 100 yards from the operation room, he never would have survived!

We learned that DJ's heart had begun working harder and harder every day. The cardiologist compared it to a constant jog at rest—and a full sprint when he was moderately active. DJ wasn't able to take in enough nourishment and, to make things worse, he developed severe reflux. The esophageal sphincter was open and would not close properly, so he was throwing up half of what he ate. The only solution was a surgery called a fundoplication. This surgery wraps the upper portion of the stomach around the bottom of the esophagus. At the time of DJ's surgery, this was a full surgery—he was cut from his belly button up to his chest. It is common in cardiac patients to place a tube from the stomach, through the stomach wall, which exits a few inches above the belly button.

The benefits of continuous overnight feedings and the ease of administering medications without swallowing would make caring for DJ simpler. The fact that we did not have to put the NG tube down his little nose feeding it into his stomach anymore was truly a weight lifted. It had gotten so bad for poor DJ that his nasal passages and throat were always irritated. This G-tube meant relief for him.

In the midst of it all, our thoughts turned to our eldest son, Derek. He and DJ were bosom buddies and had full-fledged conversations on a variety of topics, but often about the Lord and heaven. We had committed both the boys to our Heavenly Father and trusted Him explicitly with their lives and ours.

We also realized that, if DJ passed away, Derek would have a huge emotional hole of lost brotherly love and his big-brother relationship. It was then we decided to have a third child. The problem was Linda's physical condition, statistics and our doctors' concerns. She had some internal damage from DJ's quick delivery. In retrospect, the fast birth put less stress on his heart and is probably how he survived his birth—but it increased the trauma to Linda's body. If that wasn't enough of a deterrent, the probability of having another child with a heart defect doubled after DJ's birth, so the doctors' rigorously discouraged more progeny.

Sometimes, you need to do what is right for your children and trust in the promises of God. He controls the womb and we asked Him to allow Linda to get pregnant, if that was best for our future. David Robert Blechinger was born February 26, 1992, perfectly healthy—and then there were three comancheros! Our three boys were here—just as I had predicted five years earlier.

DJ loved being a big brother! (In the back of this book are some photos. Find the one of DJ holding David in his lap and you will see the proudest big brother ever!)

A year after David's birth, I took a job with Scientific-Atlanta. We were having a house built in Auburn, Georgia, moving from the south side to the north side. I commuted 65 miles one way for six months while the house was being built.

So let's recap on the stress-o-meter: a chronically ill son, a new baby, a new job and the building of a new home, then the move. Whew! On the list of most stressful experiences in life, all of these are in the top 10. So how did I withstand pressure that creates diamonds from coal? Was it my iron will? My strict self-discipline? Superhuman strength? The answer is "no" to all of the above.

There is not one righteous, no not one.

No one can overcome the onslaught of tribulations alone. Our wills are weak. We lack and reject discipline of any kind and humanity is morally bankrupt, folding under minimal opposition. The only way I survived—the only way I could go on, day after day—was by tapping into a source of unlimited power. I would run to God, by reading scripture, praying constantly, seeking Him through tears and trusting in Him, regardless of my circumstances. The simple fact is none of us are going to get out of this thing called "life" alive. Life is precious, but everything that has a beginning has an end.

You've got to make a choice and a commitment in your heart. You either really believe or you don't. If you really believe, then you better live it, through faith—and that is when God shows you He is real, shows Himself as real, and reveals Himself to you.

Jesus Christ is the Alpha and the Omega. He has no beginning and no end. That's why He's eternal and is forever. I know that what I'm about to tell you may seem backward. I am hoping that being transparent and showing my weakness will encourage you. I am 100 percent human. I am frail. I screw up all the time. I struggle in the purity of my thought life. I sometimes curse when I get hurt and when I get mad. I am far from perfect.

Sometimes, I'm smart and take the appropriate action, immediately. Other times, I get prideful and it takes a swift kick in the rear, after days or weeks, before I act. I run to the Cross. I admit my sin, ask for forgiveness and repent. That is being a real man and that is how you shed all the pressures of life. Realize it is not your life anymore—it's His and He has every right to do with you whatever He likes. The same goes for your wife, your children and everything you think you own. It's all His, anyway—we are just stewards for a time.

Someone once told us, "God has entrusted the two of you with great responsibility." What a perspective! These children are not punishment. The illnesses are not punishment. God has entrusted us. He is relying upon us to take good care of one of His little ones. It's like someone handing you the most precious thing in life and putting it in your hands to protect. That is what God did, when he gave me a wife and then children through her.

When DJ was about 3, he came to a point where we had a break from the constant barrage of surgeries. On occasion, our mothers came to Newnan to help out. Then, a winter wonderland trip to New York ended abruptly as DJ's health failed, due to the frigid conditions of the Snow Belt. We had to be extremely careful of his exposure to environment, people and the transfer of viruses, but he was pretty healthy and became a little mobile unit.

Reluctantly, Linda and I agreed to put DJ on the heart transplant list. Our expectations that he would receive a new heart were very low. New hearts for children are hard to come by and just the thought of another baby having to die to provide this solution was unfathomable to us and seemed morbid. Fortunately (and unfortunately), DJ had extremely high antibodies from all the surgeries. He had also picked up Hepatitis C from one of his many blood transfusions, so the probability of rejecting the heart was high, putting him at the bottom of the list.

He finally had enough strength to walk without the assistance of the baby walker and we tried to enjoy the façade of being a normal family. We were assigned a beeper, but focused on embracing every moment, instead of banking our hope on a long-shot donor. Evidence of his heart condition had already taken a toll on his physique. In addition to the scars that covered his entire body, he was nothing but skin and bone. His heart was working so hard that it burned every ounce of nourishment we pumped into his stomach over a continuous eight-hour period every night. He had a bluish tint, due to a low oxygenation percentage in his bloodstream, and that only became more pronounced with any type of activity. The same condition caused clubbing in his extremities, the enlarging of his fingertips and toes.

Our baby David was a Hoss and, at a year old, he already weighed more than his big brother. I would typically carry David on outings and Linda carried DJ. But, when DJ wanted to go fast and have the thrill of speed, I would give him a piggyback ride in high gear. I would run and he would laugh. He was the typical child when it came to having fun.

"Do it again, Daddy," he'd say. I would run until totally exhausted, but he was instantly ready for another lap around the house, before I could catch my breath. DJ loved to swing, go down the slide and play in the lawn sprinkler but, by far, his favorite outdoor activity was the piggyback ride.

🐉 CHAPTER ELEVEN
HOW DO YOU SAY GOOD-BYE?

DJ's energy level decreased slowly over the next year to a point where getting up and walking from his bedroom to the living room would exhaust him. We had come to a crossroads. He was on a decline and would go into heart failure, unless we took the doctors' recommendation and moved forward with the only other option—another open-heart surgery.

The last surgery was the most invasive: The Fontan was the all-or-nothing surgery. Surgeons would correct the transposition of the great arteries and close the hole previously created between the two sides of the heart. This procedure would be his last. It would completely correct the structure of the heart, and there were no other alternatives.

The day before the surgery, I put DJ on my back and headed out the front door. I wanted him to feel the wind on his face one last time, but he couldn't hold on, so I cradled him and started to run. I had it in my mind that, no matter how many times he said that old familiar phrase, "Do it again, Daddy," I would go again, until my legs fell off. Before I could get up to a full sprint, I heard, "Daddy stop, please stop!" My heart sank as we went back into the house without taking one lap.

The surgery the next day took eight hours and, when he came into CICU, he looked the worst ever. He had multiple chest tubes to drain fluid from his abdomen and IVs and wires to more monitors than a computer room.

I took account of his past four years and was amazed at his resolve. I mean, how much physical punishment could a human baby withstand? When he became conscious, there was no forced smile after the surgery like before. He was tired, spent, and the fight was gone. The chest tubes could not be removed, because his heart had operated at such a low pressure that the walls of the heart never became thickened. The proper structure made the pressures normal and the blood was pushing through the heart walls into his chest. He was in CICU for 52 days, with a short three-day trip home and then immediately back to the hospital.

His condition was not improving and Linda and I held the doctors to our agreement. Before DJ went into this surgery, Dr. Ravielle and Dr. Kanter explained thoroughly what we could expect from the procedure: where the critical turning points would be, how the heart may or may not respond and, if things went south, the chilling fact that all of our options were gone. This was all or nothing. After taking in the finality of the discussion, we proposed an agreement and they accepted it: If there was nothing left that medical science could do for him, they would let us take DJ home. These men had grown to love our DJ, his joyous spirit and his love of life. They had joined in his fight for life and did not want to give in or give up for his sake. But the time had come, the proverbial die was cast and there was nothing left in this world that could help him.

The doctors were good to their word and DJ came home on my wife's 35th birthday—March 3rd, 1995. He was weak as a newborn kitten. We fitted out his room with a huge oxygen machine and tried to make him as comfortable as possible. We would not give up the hope of a miracle. I'm unbelievably practical, but God is able to do anything. Prayer was our staple, as it had been since his birth.

We began our nightly prayers with the boys: "Jesus, Our Lord and Savior, we trust and love you. We know you have the power to heal and pray that You will give DJ the strength to get better . . . "

"Daddy, stop," said DJ, interrupting the prayer. I was concerned and began to check on his physical condition.

"Are you OK, DJ?" I asked him.

"Yes, but please stop praying that way."

"What way, buddy?"

"For me to get better," said DJ. "I want to be with Jesus."

It was like a searing hot knife through my very soul. Jesus was an integral part of our lives. In fact, He was, is and always will be our very lives. But I had to pray for DJ's healing. I was his Dad and surely it was my responsibility to intercede on his behalf to place these petitions at the feet of Christ in His Throne. I needed to be the persistent widow, to keep asking until God relented and fulfilled my request. I'd have the doctors tether DJ's pulmonary system to mine and carry him on my back. I would cut out my heart for him to continue on. He was purer than I, more worthy of life. He loved people more openly than I did and loved Jesus without any reservation or doubt.

"What?!" was all that came out of my mouth, as tears began to flow from Linda, Derek and my eyes.

"Daddy, pray for me to go and be with Jesus," our little boy requested.

It was one of the hardest things I've ever had to do. The hope to which I had been clinging for almost five years was gone. All I had before me was my little man's request.

"Jesus, comfort DJ. Prepare him to enter into Your presence. He's done fighting. He has finished the race You set before him, and is ready to be with You," I prayed.

DJ was a special soul. I had seen his faith in action his whole life—from Derek and him preaching to passersby from the front steps to this final act of committing his soul into His hands for eternity.

We had no idea how long DJ could hold on. I returned to work and, by week's end, the call that I had been dreading came from my wife.

"Dan, get home quickly," she said. "I don't know how much longer DJ will be with us."

There are critical decisions in life—times when a choice can destroy your life or at least position you to be able to live with yourself. I knew my wife and children—especially DJ—needed me so, without hesitation and as quickly and safely as possible, I headed home. I did not have any other thoughts, because there was no way I could live with myself if I went and hid in a bottle. I want to encourage you Dads—be there, no matter the circumstances, as long as it is possible!

I arrived home and DJ was in his bed, still breathing. In short order, my sister Kim and Randy showed up and then Carl Greene, our dear friend and pastor from Newnan. Linda had coordinated with Kim to keep Derek and David during this time. Derek was almost 6 and David was 3. It was not really a scene for children this young. Before leaving, they went in to say goodbye to DJ. Kim began singing a lullaby, which he typically loved, but all he wanted was peace and quiet, so he softly asked Kim to stop. After a final farewell and short prayer, they headed back to Cartersville with Derek and David.

Carl was there for Linda and me, particularly for intercessory pray on our behalf.

Occasionally, DJ would stop breathing and then jump, like a person startling when falling to sleep. His adrenaline would kick in and so would mine, leaving both of us wide eyed. He couldn't get comfortable and hated the oxygen mask, but it was necessary.

Before the hospice nurse was dismissed, she told us not to give him anything to eat or drink, because his organs were shutting down. Still, when DJ asked Linda for a drink of Sprite, no request was too great and Linda brought in a full 8-ounce cup of DJ's favorite soda. Even when DJ was at his best, he could not swallow a large quantity of liquid, due to his enlarged heart and the fundoplication. To our astonishment, he downed the entire drink in one breath and gave a satisfying exhale of complete satisfaction.

He then wanted to move onto Mom and Dad's warm waterbed, so we rigged up the portable oxygen tank and put him in the middle of the king-sized bed. Now he could hardly roll over on his side, due to weakness, and struggled to raise his head. He wanted us to lay down with him on the bed, so we did. DJ sat up in bed without any assistance, took off his mask and let out a load roar. Linda and I looked at each other with disbelief over what had just happened. But then he lay back down, rolled over on his left side with his head on my right shoulder and his right leg draped over my right leg.

Stillness came over us, and the three of us fell into a deep slumber. I woke up to Linda crying. She whispered, "He is gone." He was still laying on me. I put my hand on his back and discovered he had passed. I began to wail.

The five years of pushing down all the emotions came to the surface in a flood and overwhelmed any self composure. I let loose and didn't care who would hear. The spirit of peace that had descended on our home had caused Carl to also sleep, but all of the commotion brought him from his nap into our bedroom in a hurry. He assessed the scene and immediately joined us in mourning.

DJ's race ended on March 13, 1995, and he ran it well right to the finish.

Carl contacted the coroner. He arrived and I carried DJ's lifeless body, wrapped in his own blanket, outside to the hearse. Linda and I said our goodbyes, but he wasn't there with us, anymore. His prayer had been answered. He was with Jesus. We locked up the house and headed for Cartersville to be with our other sons.

The Aftermath

Everyone would agree that the worse experience in a person's life is to bury his or her own child. Carl made all the arrangements, after we selected Newnan as the location for the funeral. He did a fantastic job honoring DJ in the service. He took everyone through an emotional roller coaster of the events of DJ's life, from laughter to tears and back. At times, he would tear up, but quickly regain his composure. I, on the other hand, was a basket case. I was crushed by the grief. Any pride I had left and any emotional control was purged and I was laid bare before the overflow crowd in the sanctuary as I wept. Carl guided us through the procession, the graveside committal and the burial. I know I was there, but the details escape me. It is all a blur of emotions and memories.

The first major holiday after DJ's passing was Easter. We had a house full of family and among them were my eldest sister Lyn and her husband Tom, who drove down from Virginia. Now I love my sister but, when she starting instructing me on how to grieve, I took exception. I understand that, during her visit, she had not seen any emotional expression of grief and she was genuinely concerned for my wellbeing, but it wasn't anyone else's place to define.

Here is the message of this little conflict: Everyone grieves differently. My experiences will be different than yours and, even when your experiences are the same, as was true for me and Linda, everyone reacts differently to stress, conflict and events in thought and emotion. The relationship you have with the one for whom you're grieving will be different.

In this particular situation, here were the conditions:

Over 30 days had passed since the funeral.

I had a house full of people celebrating the resurrection of Christ.

I had emotional outbursts all the time, but usually it was only when alone.

A person has a choice of in whose presence to bare their soul.

Your grief is your own and mourning is personal and unique. You should mourn how you wish—but do mourn in your way. Don't bottle it up and suppress all those emotions. That is another one of those choices that can destroy you. I am not telling you how, when or where—I'm just saying the only way to continue life is by allowing yourself to go through the grieving process. I know that was also the intent of my sister's good-hearted nudging.

I had a laundry list of continuing struggles.

The worst was that I felt relieved. DJ was no longer a constant focus of attention—no more medicines every four hours, no more overnight feedings with soaked sheets because the tube had pulled loose, no more anticipation of phone calls, beepers, doctors' visits or emergency trips to the hospital.

This feeling of relief quickly turned into a feeling of guilt. How could I feel relief? That was wrong and I told myself that surely I was a horrible father if I felt a release, a freedom by his death.

As usual, I turned to the Holy Bible to seek an answer. I read a passage in II Samuel Chapter 12. In it, King David had committed several sins to get himself in a predicament that differed from my circumstances. Bathsheba had conceived an illegitimate son by David. David had seen Bathsheba and desired her, so David sent her loyal husband Uriah to the war front to die.

What we had in common, though, was a child who was at death's door. David wept and prayed, but his child died. David cleaned himself up, went into the house of the Lord to worship and then went to eat. His servants were surprised and a little put off and upset with the King.

21 *Then his servants said to him, "What is this thing you have done? While the child was alive, you fasted and wept; but when the child died, you arose and ate food."*

22 *And he said, "While the child was still alive, I fasted and wept; for I said, 'Who knows, the Lord may be gracious to me, that the child may live.'*

23 But now he has died; why should I fast? Can I bring him back again? I shall go to him, but he will not return to me."

The effort, caring and investment of time is only of value while the loved one is alive. The relief is natural and God intended it to be that way. It's not that the memories are erased or the emotions of the experience are gone, but we have to continue with life. If we could not let go, we would not be able to help anyone. We would have a world of people consumed with grief so introspective that they would be unable to help anyone, influence or minister to people in the world outside of themselves.

Catch that last sentence in verse 23, *"I shall go to him, but he will not return to me."*

David knew the newborn was with God and, when David died, he would be with God and with his son. I took great comfort in this passage, knowing DJ was in God's care and that, someday, I would be able to be with him, again.

Another scripture verse that clarified my perspective is the one that describes when Moses is before the burning bush. God says, from within the fire, *"I am the God of Abraham, Isaac, and Jacob, I am the God of the living and not the dead."*

I am amazed at how direct God is in proclaiming eternal life. He lists the first three Patriarchs and essentially tells us, "These guys are still alive and in My presence, worshipping Me right now as their God."

This eternal perspective is paramount in understanding the meaning and purpose of life on earth, as well as eternal life. There is a faithful saying: "This life is the worst it gets for Christians—and the best it gets for unbelievers."

If you truly believe there is a God and His Son, Jesus Christ, was born of a virgin, lived a sinless life and sacrificed Himself for your personal sins, then ask for His forgiveness and invite Him into your life, you will be saved.

Children, from the point of conception to the age of ascension, are guaranteed entrance into heaven. So, if you had a child who was too young to have mental ascent and understand these concepts before they died, they will be with God in Heaven. King David's son was a newborn. He did not have the mental capacity to make a choice of accepting Jesus, and he could not comprehend the tenets of the Christian faith.

God would have it that not one should perish—no, not one. This is not my personal, wishful thinking. This is a fact and a promise from God Almighty. It's not how long you live on the planet; it's how many lives you've touched with the love of Christ. This is the ultimate purpose and goal of life!

A lesser guilt that I confronted was my pattern of revisiting every decision I had made. I was second guessing every choice, from DJ's birth until his death. I'd rethink every situation, every decision point, every critical choice, over and over again. I was driving myself crazy, trying to figure out where I went wrong.

Here's the problem: It was over and in the past. Sorry, but you can't turn back the clock and change the choices. Even if I had discovered a mistake, there is no way to go back and fix it. When I finally accepted that, I realized my future choices are what matter.

Living with the past and choosing to love my wife more and better, pouring my life into my two surviving children and placing greater importance on helping them deal with the loss was the key.

Being introspective and retrospective can be beneficial practices for mental health and application to future decisions, but you can't stay in either of those states. The light of life comes from the outside. Shutting yourself off from the outside only fills the inner self and the past with darkness. The important thing is letting yourself deal with the inner conflicts, laying them to rest by trusting that God is sovereign, and moving back to the outside and reestablishing connections to loved ones and your future. The process is a difficult and painful one, but the passage through the valley of the shadow of death is a necessary one.

To top off all of the negative feelings, I was not very happy with God. In fact, I was downright mad at Him. I questioned His motives, His reasoning for DJ's heart defects and why DJ could not have been born healthy, instead of my family going through hell on earth. Frankly, I didn't think it was fair. I was far from perfect, but I wasn't like King David—or was I?

I started looking at the results in my own life. I am not implying that DJ was born with birth defects because of my sins—past, present or future. I know Christ died for me on the cross and His blood has taken away all my sins. I also know that our Father God chastises His children, who He loves but it is the kindness of God that leads to repentance. Even though I was angry with Him, I knew who God was and who He wasn't, and that He is a big God and could take whatever I threw at Him.

I wanted answers and God was more than willing to give them. The question was whether I really wanted to know. Could I receive and accept His answers?

Before DJ's birth, I was more concerned with my career than my family. Growing up, I had no father figure. I was wild, immature and full of youthful ignorance, selfishness and self-righteousness that many people would call stupidity. And that was fine with me, because I held the world in contempt. I cared more about tasks and getting things done than people's plights, struggles, emotions and needs. My attitude was "Your problems are your problems and not my problems. You had an emotional, traumatic life experience. Get over it, move on and get the job done."

After DJ's life and death, I was no longer that egotistical, arrogant, insensitive young man. God had taught me how to be a good husband, a good father, a good friend, and a good leader who would no longer be callous to people in need. He had done a great work in me. My anger turned into understanding, but the emotional scars were deep and it would take time for them to heal.

Fortunately, God is very patient. In the last book of the Bible, God burns up the old earth with fire and creates a new heaven and earth. In the new Heaven is the Tree of Life. The Bible says the leaves of the tree are for the healing of the nations. I interpret that to mean some hurts are so deep that they cannot be healed until we get to Heaven. Even so, we should seek healing in our lives as much as possible while here on earth.

Debt was another crushing force. We had good insurance, but the 80/20 split still left a hefty sum to pay. Twenty percent of a $100,000 surgery is still 20 grand. String seven of those together and, like I said, it's a pretty hefty sum—not to mention owing the pharmacy almost 10 thousand dollars. I liquidated my 401K with Photocircuits and then my 401K with Scientific-Atlanta, but that only took care of maybe 25 percent.

We were drowning in debt and I'd lie if I said it wasn't affecting my marriage. Linda handled dealing with the insurance processing and it was a royal pain, thanks to the constant coding mistakes by the processors and the incessant badgering by the collection agencies.

One day, Mr. Goodman of Goodman Pharmacy sent me a bill that said, "Paid in Full." I called him, because I knew we owed him a good sum of money and he must have made a mistake. John had been allowing us to pay on-time installments without interest, which I greatly appreciated. His reply? "It has been taken care of, Mr. Blechinger." I thanked him profusely.

After I hung up the phone, I dropped to my knees, thanked God for the blessing and proceeded to request a ten-fold blessing for Mr. Goodman for his generosity. One can only fathom that, over the almost five years of DJ's life, he had plucked some of John's heart strings. Only a heart of compassion cancels a debt like that!

One by one, the bills arrived, marked "Paid in Full," with letters from doctors telling us the debt was taken care of—usually by some anonymous source!

But, you see, that is the power of God. He changes the hearts of people and truly concerns Himself with the affairs of mankind. I was fully committed to paying off the bills, even if it took the rest of my lifetime. These were real debts I had created by pursuing life for my son. No one had forced me, and the doctors and hospitals were not obligated to save his life. I wanted and asked them to do the surgeries and administer the medicines. I was not entitled to a free pass, but God, through his mercy and grace, freed me from those debts! I never felt like I deserved it or that God owed it to me, but thankfulness was always on my lips.

The Sun Also Rises

Where was the laughter? Where were the songs and lullabies? Our home, once filled with happiness, became a solemn and dull place. I could muster a fake smile or chuckle, but my heart was filled with sorrow and I knew that life would never be the same without DJ.

Then July 30, DJ's birthday, rolled around four short months after the funeral. Linda came up with an idea: We would write DJ notes, tie them to helium balloons and launch them into the summer sky. Our boys loved the idea and we conducted a little family ceremony to commemorate the occasion. Every year, we would have some little remembrance. One year, a birthday cake; another year, a trip to the graveside for prayer. Every year, we would honor him through memories.

As life went on, the events of living nudged sorrow out of the way and the gloominess in a corner of my heart was replaced with a ray of light. Watching one of the boys playing a baseball or football game, going on family vacations, playing board games at night, watching a good movie together, or praying with the boys before bed all contributed to the end of the deep mourning. There were occasions when a song, circumstance or situation would arise that would remind us of DJ—something he would have loved to see or experience. I would hear his unique little laugh in my mind and a flood of emotions would wash over me.

But the joy of having known him began to replace the searing grief of living without him.

In the summer of 2004, we had a Blechinger family reunion, back in my hometown of Pulaski, New York. Everyone who could come did and those who could not attend were missed. It was nine years after DJ's death. Randy's brother, Bobby, was a praise-and-worship leader for a local church and everyone coerced him into bringing his guitar to the house we rented for the occasion. We started singing worship songs and praising God and thanking Him for His goodness and loving kindness. I was singing in harmony with Bobby and looked over at my wife, who had the biggest smile on her face. I was dancing.

She knew God had done something special right at that moment to replace my mourning with joy. The change manifested itself in my body. I hadn't even realized my feet were moving to the music! The sun had finally risen in my heart and joy and hope entered back in.

Linda and I have both had dreams and visions. I'm a little jealous, because hers have involved DJ, but not as a baby. She has seen him as an adolescent and as a full-grown man. In her visions, he's not a baby anymore.

God gives each of us what we need to move from mourning into the morning of the new dawn. Life is filled with many sorrows that you will never forget, but the sharp edges of the bad memories are dulled and the good memories are what eventually come to the forefront of your mind more often than the bad. The Holy Spirit will reveal meaning in the events and the value of a precious one who passed, so that you can share with others who are going through similar pain.

One such encouragement was given to me regarding DJ's final drink of Sprite and roar. You may recall that, an hour before he died, DJ asked for a drink and emptied the entire contents of the cup with great satisfaction. Then, right before death, he sat up and roared.

It seemed curious to me and so, one day, I asked the Lord for illumination. This is what I received.

At the cross, Jesus asked for a drink. He then entered into Paradise and Abraham's bosom to lead the host of captives free from the grip of death and the grave. DJ shared in that victory over the grave and was toasting to that success—the new blood covenant Christ had made with mankind to give us eternal life!

Scripture also says Satan goes about like a roaring lion, seeking who he may devour. DJ met that old serpent head on, without fear, and roared right back in his face! DJ knew Satan was a defeated foe and Christ was more powerful—He is the Lion of The Tribe Of Judah, the King of Kings and the Lord of Lords.

I pray that each of us Christians will have that much faith and confidence when we cross that threshold and enter into Eternity!

Conclusion:

I want to leave you with Proverbs 3. Please read it, drawing as many parallels from this book as possible and realizing this one thing: Although each of our lives is unique, my journey and your journey are on the exact same road. God is trying to teach all of His children the same truths.

Everything shared within these pages are summed up in this:

1. *My son, do not forget my teaching,*
   But let your heart keep my commandments;
2. *For length of days and years of life*
   And peace they will add to you.
3. *Do not let kindness and truth leave you;*
   Bind them around your neck,
   Write them on the tablet of your heart.
4. *So you will find favor and good repute*
   In the sight of God and man.
5. *Trust in the LORD with all your heart*
   And do not lean on your own understanding.
6. *In all your ways acknowledge Him,*
   And He will make your paths straight.
7. *Do not be wise in your own eyes;*
   Fear the LORD and turn away from evil.
8. *It will be healing to your body*
   And refreshment to your bones.
9. *Honor the LORD from your wealth*
   And from the first of all your produce;
10. *So your barns will be filled with plenty*
    And your vats will overflow with new wine.
11. *My son, do not reject the discipline of the LORD*
    Or loathe His reproof,
12. *For whom the LORD loves He reproves,*
    Even as a father corrects the son in whom he delights.
13. *How blessed is the man who finds wisdom*
    And the man who gains understanding.
14. *For her profit is better than the profit of silver*
    And her gain better than fine gold.

15. *She is more precious than jewels;*
    And nothing you desire compares with her.
16. *Long life is in her right hand;*
    In her left hand are riches and honor.
17. *Her ways are pleasant ways*
    And all her paths are peace.
18. *She is a tree of life to those who take hold of her,*
    And happy are all who hold her fast.
19. *The LORD by wisdom founded the earth,*
    By understanding He established the heavens.
20. *By His knowledge the deeps were broken up*
    And the skies drip with dew.
21. *My son, let them not vanish from your sight;*
    Keep sound wisdom and discretion,
22. *So they will be life to your soul*
    And adornment to your neck.
23. *Then you will walk in your way securely*
    And your foot will not stumble.
24. *When you lie down, you will not be afraid;*
    When you lie down, your sleep will be sweet.
25. *Do not be afraid of sudden fear*
    Nor of the onslaught of the wicked when it comes;
26. *For the LORD will be your confidence*
    And will keep your foot from being caught.
27. *Do not withhold good from those to whom it is due,*
    When it is in your power to do it.
28. *Do not say to your neighbor, "Go, and come back,*
    And tomorrow I will give it,"
    When you have it with you.
29. *Do not devise harm against your neighbor,*
    While he lives securely beside you.
30. *Do not contend with a man without cause,*
    If he has done you no harm.
31. *Do not envy a man of violence|*
    And do not choose any of his ways.
32. *For the devious are an abomination to the LORD;*
    But He is intimate with the upright.
33. *The curse of the LORD is on the house of the wicked,*
    But He blesses the dwelling of the righteous.

34. *Though He scoffs at the scoffers,*
    Yet He gives grace to the afflicted.
35. *The wise will inherit honor,*
    But fools display dishonor.

May the Lord bless you and keep you, may He lift up His countenance upon you and give you peace.

CHAPTER TWELVE
WAYS TO HELP IN TIMES
OF GRIEF

I do not have all the answers. I have made my share of mistakes and blunders. These are simply suggestions. Some of these may work for you; some may not.

When friends helped us or sent notes, I found these loving gestures really ministered to me. Also, in speaking with family and friends, they have offered some further suggestions.

If you know someone who is experiencing loss, please don't hesitate to write letters or notes. My suggestion is try not to say you understand; instead, write a letter of remembrance to the family. Honor the person and let them know that person impacted you. Perhaps you have a sweet or funny story you could share with the family.

Respect the family's needs. Some people are very private and want to grieve alone in their own homes, while others need people around. You can ask what would be helpful. Most people will tell you what they need if you ask.

I try to send live plants instead of cut flowers to the funeral parlor or home. When flowers die, it is sad to throw them away.

Mark the anniversary date on your calendar and send a small note telling the person you are thinking of them at this time.

As stated throughout the book, please just let them cry. Let them withdraw for a time. Calling every once in awhile or sending notes are good reminders that they have people who care about them.

If you are available to help logistically during the funeral, offer to help coordinate food for the family, or pick up out-of-town guests that might be arriving for the funeral. Relatives might also need lodging.

There may be a lot of children around during the wake or funeral. You might offer to keep the little ones at your house during one of those periods.

If you have pictures of the person who passed away, it is nice to receive a copy with a note of remembrance.

Sending a card with money for meals or relief is helpful. A friend of mine sent a card to a family that has several children; the oldest one took the younger ones out for a while. It was good for everyone.

Finances are usually an issue. However, please realize any giving to the family should be done discreetly, perhaps through a relative or church.

I think it is important to remember that, during the time of grieving, most people have nothing emotionally to give. If you aren't able to hold it together, don't visit or call until you are ready. You want to encourage them. Send a note instead of visiting.

Be patient. People who are grieving don't always respond to the immediate. I remember about two or three months after the funeral, sitting down and reading through cards, crying and rejoicing in the things that were conveyed about DJ. It was a real blessing to me.

Several people sent or brought us trees to honor DJ. We loved this tribute. Ten years later, we watch them come to life every spring.

Some Thoughts on Self Help

I write "self help," but what I really mean is God helping me. These are some of the things I personally did during the first year after DJ's passing and beyond:

I read God's word. Even when I didn't feel like it, I did it. I read through the Psalms very often. I wrote out promises and posted them all around my house—on my refrigerator, my bathroom mirror, anywhere I went consistently.

I kept tapes in the car of worship music. I found a beautiful CD called "The Golden City," all about heaven.

I wrote in my journal. I cried—a lot. I went for walks and I always brought tissues. I walked my dog Abby. I held her and cried to her as I stroked her. She was really safe; I knew I wasn't adding to her grief, yet she was warm and alive and comforting to me.

One day, Derek was in school and David was napping. I went out on my back deck and screamed as loud as I could. I cried passionately, sobbing as I spoke to God, "Why did you take him? You know my heart is broken. I can't make it. Why Father, why?"

In my heart, I heard God's soft gentle voice: "I know you are hurting. I hurt with you. I love you, Linda, and I love DJ. He is fine now, all healed up. He is happy." Somehow that was enough for the day. I went back in and washed up. I was OK. It is good to know God doesn't mind us questioning him. He knows we are full of pain, hurt and questions. He is a big God. He can deal with it and really He is the only one to whom we can run in times of trouble. I recall and rehearse the Names of God. There is a verse Psalm 9:10 that says, "And those who know Thy name will put their trust in Thee; for Thou O LORD hast not forsaken those who seek Thee." I have written on the inside of my Bible cover many of the Names of God, along with their references in scripture. You see, in the Hebrew language, every time God revealed Himself to His people, He was addressed by the name that denoted His character, who He is and what He has done. It is truly beautiful to study the names of God. As in any relationship, the more time you spend with a person, the better you know them. The same applies to our God.

Here are some of the Names of God I called on in my days of trouble:

El Elyon—The God Most High
El Roi—God Who Sees
El Shaddai—The All-Sufficient One
Adonai—LORD, Master
Jehovah-Shaloam—The LORD is Peace
Jehovah—Shammah—The LORD Is There
El Olam—The Everlasting God
Jehovah-rapha—The LORD Who Heals

Call on God, my friend. He is there for you, He loves you and He hasn't forgotten you in your day of trouble. He is your very present help in time of need.

Mistakes I Made

I tried too quickly to start doing things outside the home. At the time of DJ's death, we did not yet belong to a church. We had just moved to the north side of Atlanta five months before. We had visited a few churches before DJ passed away, but hadn't settled on one, yet. We began to visit again, but I just couldn't do it. Every time the choir started to sing, I would begin sobbing. Sometimes, we had to leave. I just wasn't ready for this.

As summer approached, I went to enroll the boys in VBS at a church close by. I was asked if I wanted to help. I thought it would be good for the boys and me, so I said yes. When I got home, I started doubting I could really do this. I thought, "Three months has passed; I should be able to do this." I basically talked myself into it. Bad idea. The first day, I saw a 4-year-old boy that looked like DJ. I lost it, and the flood gates opened. I didn't go back to serve—I couldn't. In time, I was able but, at that point, it was too soon.

I began comforting myself with food, which is really easy for me to do. I love to cook and bake and I always had my three guys who never objected to food! I ate and ate. I then hated myself for overeating. It was a vicious cycle. When we eat food high in sugar and fat, it really does cause blood-sugar highs and lows. I was adding to the problem, not helping. Walking instead of eating, reading, praying—choose something healthy, not destructive.

I made mistakes in judging what I was capable of participating in. I remember I said I would attend a wedding. It was a special person whom I loved but, when the time drew near, I couldn't do it. I then felt like such a failure. I let my friend down and I was miserable, but it was too much of a connection for me with DJ. I kept thinking I would never see him walk down the aisle. It started a whole progression of thoughts. That was another part of the process for me. I didn't have anyone to ask me, "Linda, are you sure you are ready for this?" I thought I was weak and not a strong Christian. Condemnation came upon me. I sank lower and lower. I share all of this, not because I expect you will face all the same feelings and emotions, but because I want you to know it was hard. It was a progression of healing. My heart was broken and it would just take time and the events of life to bring true healing. God doesn't waste anything and, as it turned out, I was asked to share my testimony about DJ several times. Every time I did share, it became a part of the healing process. Every time I spoke was a milestone.

Time and again, I would go back to the scripture from Isaiah that spoke of the refiner's fire. I learned that a silversmith must heat the silver over and over again. Seven times he heats it and, every time he does, impurities rise to the surface and he skims them off. He knows when the silver is truly refined—when he looks into the liquid silver and can see his own refection! Yes, that is God our Faithful Father—He is skimming off the impurities. Through every trial, the things in me that are not godly, holy and righteous are skimmed off. I keep trying to do it on my own and, when I fail, He is there to pick me up, brush me off and show me truth. I had to learn I can do all things through Christ who strengthens me.

He has a perfect plan for our lives, for our healing. He will walk us through it and bring us to the other side. *Even though I walk through the valley of the shadow of death, I fear no evil, for You are with me; Your rod and Your staff they comfort me.* Psalm23:4. I had to learn this: God is with me, He does comfort me and evil will not overtake me. God's guidance and Sovereignty will bring me to Him and I will be comforted, and so will you.

A Burden of GUILT

I wanted to talk about guilt, because I know what Dan and I went through in dealing with guilt, and what others have faced.

When DJ died, there was a sense of relief. Now, when I say this, I don't mean I consciously thought, "Whew! Glad that's over." No, it was deep down inside. I knew DJ was so weary of fighting. Dan and I and the boys were growing weary in those last months, physically tired and emotionally spent. There was a sense of relief that it was over—the battle was over and we were like battle weary soldiers. It was months later that I remembered that sense of relief and guilt struck—sickening guilt. It began to grow. My mind would think back to every situation where I had to make a decision and I began questioning my every choice.

I allowed myself go over to the other side, the side of emotional darkness. In the side of darkness, there is no light. The darkness changes your perspective and you can't see things clearly. All the emotions become entangled with accusations and suddenly I felt like I was plummeting down, free falling into darkness.

I ran to the Lord and pleaded, "Help me. Let me know the truth. If I caused DJ's death in some way, let me know." I had to go back to truth. I was not in control. Although I had to make decisions, DJ's life was not in my hands. Despite the surgeon's skill, DJ's life was not in his hands. My love for DJ knew no bounds; if I could have given him my life, I would have. I had to come to terms with the fact that I couldn't save him. I couldn't prolong his days.

I believe the Lord let me see a vision then of DJ, a young man, healthy and strong. It was the same vision I had of him a year before his last surgery. Now I knew God was showing me my son in Heaven, perfect and beautiful. I had to choose to let go of my guilt. I had to choose to walk in truth and to believe what I knew was true.

🐉 CHAPTER THIRTEEN
CONCLUSION

I have asked our friend and Pastor, Bruce Rhodes from Lifeway Church, to share the salvation message. This is probably the most important part of the book, so please humor me and take time to read it.

What's your Story?

What has happened in your life so far?

Wherever you have been in the past or whatever has happened in your past is not as important as where you are going and what you will do in the future.

Today is the most important day of your life, because it is the only day that you have. You do not have yesterday; it is gone forever. And you're not promised tomorrow. With each new day come many opportunities and decisions.

The daily choices you make are being written in your life's "book." Each decision you make is important and will affect your future.

What's God plan for you?

There is good news for you! God has planned a great future for you. Here's what He says about you in His Word, "For I know the plans I have for you," says the LORD. "They are plans for good and not for disaster, to give you a future and a hope." (Jeremiah 29:11 NLT). He knows those plans and He desires to reveal those plans to you—one step at a time, one day at a time.

The central part of God's plan for you is His Son, Jesus. Jesus came to earth and said this, "My purpose is to give them a rich and satisfying life." (John 10:10b NLT) God wants you to be satisfied in life. And He knows that true satisfaction can only be found in and through accepting Jesus as your personal Savior and making Him the Lord of your life. The Prince of Peace, Jesus, becomes the peace of God that passes all understanding that guards your heart and mind from all fear when you trust Him fully and give your total life to Him.

The Bible's definition of the abundant life is a life full of the love, joy and peace of God. It is a rich, satisfying and full life. God loves you and has great things in store for you.

What will you choose?

Because God has made this life available only through a personal relationship with His Son Jesus, you must choose to believe that He is Who He said He is and then receive Him by faith. The Word of God is very clear about how to choose Jesus and experience God's plan for your life. Jesus said, "You must be born again." John 3:3,7. How you can become born again is explained in Romans 10:9-10 "If you confess with your mouth that Jesus is Lord and believe in your heart that God raised him from the dead, you will be saved. For it is by believing in your heart that you are made right with God, and it is by confessing with your mouth that you are saved."

If you would like to choose to receive Jesus as your Savior and make Him your Lord right now, you can pray a prayer like this:

"Heavenly Father, in the Name of Jesus, I present myself to You. I repent of all my sin. I receive Your forgiveness. I believe that Jesus' shed blood was enough to pay for all my sin. I confess Jesus as my Savior and ask Him to be Lord over my life. I believe it in my heart, so I say it with my mouth: "Jesus has been raised from the dead." This very moment, I make Him the Lord over my life.

Jesus, come into my heart. I believe this moment that I am saved, I say it now: "I am reborn. I am a Christian. I am a child of Almighty God."

Thank God that you are now part of the family of God and a member of the Body of Christ! You have just made the biggest and best choice in your life.

What's next?

To grow spiritually, you need to put down deep roots. Begin to read and study the Bible daily. Start with learning more about Jesus. Study the Gospel of John. Begin to pray and communicate with your Heavenly Father on a daily basis. Talk to Him just like you would anyone else. Also, you need the support of a pastor and a good local church. You should look for a strong, Bible-believing, growing church in your area. Get involved in a foundations-of-faith class in the church and learn more about the commitment that you just made and what is now available to you as a child of God.

God richly bless you as you grow in your relationship with Him!

FAMILY PHOTOS

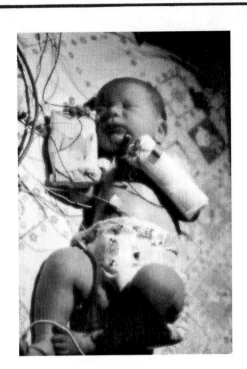

DJ Newborn

DJ 6 months

DJ 1 year

Derek 3, DJ 2, David newborn

DJ and Daddy

David and DJ

DJ 4

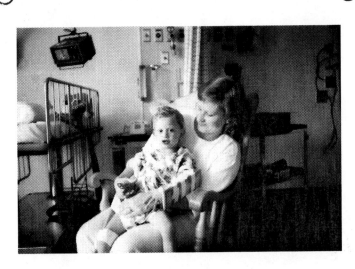

Mom and DJ

DJ 4

Aunt Kim, DJ and Derek

The Three Brothers

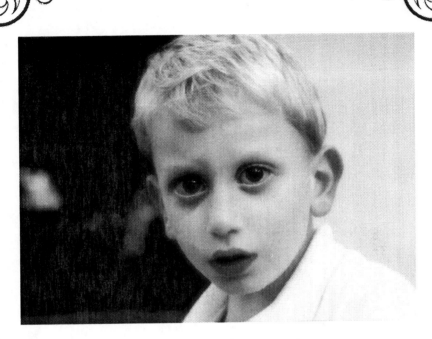

DJ 4

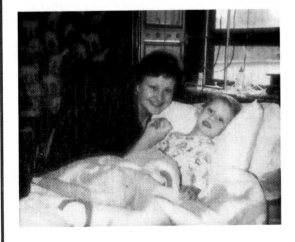

Feb 14, 1995
Last picture
with mom

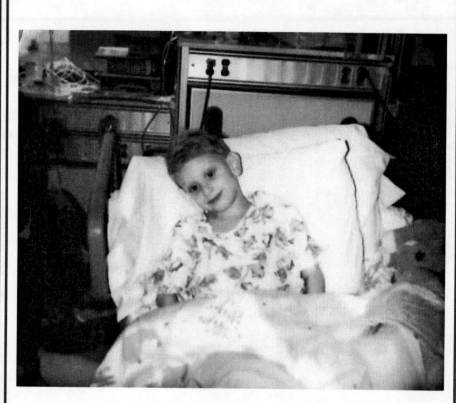

Feb. 14, 1995 Last pictures